Mammals

Amelia Bullmore

Methuen Drama

Published by Methuen Drama

1 3 5 7 9 10 8 6 4 2

First published in 2005 by
Methuen Publishing Limited

A CIP catalogue record for this book is available from
the British Library

ISBN 978-0-413-77522-1

Typeset by Country Setting, Kingsdown, Kent

The Bush Theatre presents the world premiere of

Mammals

by Amelia Bullmore
6 April – 7 May

thebushtheatre

Cast

(In order of appearance)

Jane	**Niamh Cusack**
Betty	**Helena Lymbery**
Jess	**Jane Hazlegrove**
Kev	**Daniel Ryan**
Phil	**Mark Bonnar**
Lorna	**Nancy Carroll**

Director	**Anna Mackmin**
Designer	**Paul Wills**
Lighting Design	**Howard Harrison**
Sound Design	**Mike Walker**
Assistant Director	**Alex Ferguson**
Production Manager	**John Titcombe**
Deputy Stage Manager	**Sarah Hunter**
Assistant Stage Manager	**Nafeesah Butt**

Press Representation	**Alexandra Gammie** **020 7833 2627**

Graphic Design	**Emma Cooke, Stem Design**

Mammals received its world premiere at The Bush Theatre on 8th April 2005

At The Bush Theatre

Artistic Director	**Mike Bradwell**
Executive Producer	**Fiona Clark**
General Manager	**Brenda Newman**
Literary Manager	**Abigail Gonda**
Marketing Manager	**Gillian Jones**
Technical Manager	**Matt Kirby**
Resident Stage Manager	**Ros Terry**
Acting Resident Stage Manager	**Christabel Anderson**
Literary Assistant	**Holly Hughes**
Assistant General Manager	**Nic Wass**
Box Office Supervisor	**Dominique Gerrard**
Box Office Assistants	**Rowan Bangs**
	Amanda Wright
Front of House Duty Managers	**Kellie Batchelor**
	Adrian Christopher
	Lois Tucker
	Catherine Nix-Collins
	Sarah O'Neill
Associate Artists	**Tanya Burns**
	Es Devlin
Sheila Lemon Writer in Residence	**Jennifer Farmer**
Pearson Writer in Residence	**Steve Thompson**

The Bush Theatre continues to develop its Writers Development Programme with the generous support of the Peggy Ramsay Foundation Award 2002.

The Bush Theatre
Shepherds Bush Green
London W12 8QD

The Alternative Theatre Company Ltd. (The Bush Theatre)
is a Registered Charity number: 270080
Co. registration number 1221968
VAT no. 228 3168 73

Mark Bonnar Phil

Theatre credits include *A Girl in a Car with a Man* (Royal Court), *Much Ado About Nothing* (Salisbury Playhouse), *Cyrano de Bergerac* (National Theatre), *At The Table* (Royal Court), *Twelfth Night* (Royal Exchange), *The Cherry Orchard* (Oxford Stage Company), *Robin Hood* (Caird Co. / NT Loft), *Richard III* (Sheffield Crucible), *Out in the Open* (Hampstead Theatre), *The Country Wife* (Sheffield Crucible), *Tales from Ovid* and *Volpone* (RSC), *Anthony & Cleopatra, Flight* and *Chips With Everything* (National Theatre), *Richard III* (National Studio), and *The Seal Wife* (Wimbledon Attic Theatre).

Television credits include *Afterlife* (Clerkenwell/ITV), *Taggart* (SMG), *Wire in the Blood* (Coastal/ITV), *Loving You* (Granada), *Armadillo* (BBC), *Inspector Rebus – Dead Souls* (ITV) and *The Phoenix and the Carpet* (BBC).

Nancy Carroll Lorna

Theatre credits include *The False Servant* (National Theatre), *Still Life/Astonished Heart* (Liverpool Playhouse), *A Midsummer Nights Dream* (Sheffield Crucible), *The Talking Cure* (National Theatre), *The Lady's Not For Burning* (Chichester Festival Theatre), *King Lear* (Almeida), *Henry IV parts 1 & 2, As You Like It, The Lion, the Witch and the Wardrobe* and *The Winter's Tale* (RSC) and *Hamlet* (Bristol Old Vic).

Television credits include *Midsomer Murders VIII* (Bentley Productions), *Holby* (BBC), *Cambridge Spies* (BBC), *The Gathering Storm* (BBC Films), *The Bill* (Thames) and *In Search of Shakespeare* (BBC).

Radio credits include *Rillette, Fatal Loins* and *The Family Project* (BBC).

Film credits include *Iris* (Mirimax) and *An Ideal Husband* (Ideal Film Co.).

Niamh Cusak Jane

Theatre credits include *Breathing Corpses* (Royal Court), *His Dark Materials* (National Theatre), *Nabakov's Gloves* (Hamspstead Theatre), *Indian Ink* (Aldwych), *Merchant of Venice* (Chichester Festival Theatre), *The Three Sisters* (The Gate/Royal Court), *Playboy of the Western World* (West Yorkshire Playhouse), *The Admirable Crichton* (Triumph/Haymarket), *Captain Swing* (Leeds Playhouse), *A Woman of No Importance* and *A Doll's House* (The Gate, Dublin), *As You Like It, The Art of Success, Romeo and Juliet, Othello* and *Mary After The Queen* (RSC), *The Phoenxix* (The Bush), *The Plough and Stars* (Young Vic), *The Fairy Queen* (Aix en Provence), *The Tutor* (Old Vic), *The Three Sisters* (Royal Exchange) and *Not I* (The Barbican).

Television credits include *Miss Marple* (LWT), *Too Good To Be True* (Carlton), *State of Mind* (Monogram for ITV), *Trust, Little Bird, Always and Everyone* and *Rhinoceros* (Granada), *Colour Blind* (Festival Film and TV), *Trauma* (BBC), *Heartbeat* (YTV), *Angel Train* (Granada), *Poirot, Jeeves and Wooster* and *Chalkface* (BBC), *A Marriage of Inconvenience* (Central) and *Till We Meet Again* (YTV).

Film credits include *The Closer You Get, Playboys, Shadow Under The Sun, Paris by Night, Lucky Sunil* and *Fools of Fortune*.

Jane Hazlegrove Jess

Theatre credits include *Sing Yer Heart Out for The Lads* (National Theatre), *Herons* (Royal Court), *Kes* (Royal Exchange), *Snake in the Grass* (Old Vic), *Holes in the Skin* (Chichester Festival Theatre), *Wishbones, Boom Bang-a-Bang* and *The Mortal Ash* (Bush Theatre), *Accrington Pals* (West Yorkshire Playhouse), *The Wolves* (Paines Plough/Tour), *Heartbreak House* (Coventry), *My Mother Said I Never Should, Blood Wedding* (Bolton), *Whistle Down the Wind* (Oldham), *The Crucible* (Manchester Library) and *To Kill a Mockingbird* (Manchester Contact).

Television credits include *Buried* (World Productions), *Silent Witness* (BBC), *Without Motive* (United), *The Cops* (World), *Hero To Zero* (BBC), *Making Out* (BBC), *Faith* (Company Pictures), *Dalziel and Pascoe* and *Judge John Deed* (BBC).

Film credits include *Cheeky, The Whipping Boy* and *Herbert's Balls*.

Helena Lymbery Betty

Born and raised in London, Helena trained at L.A.M.D.A.

Theatre credits include *Sleeping Beauty* (Barbican and Victory Theatre, New York), *Iphigenia at Aulis* and *His Dark Materials* (The National Theatre), *Sleeping Beauty* (Young Vic), *Blue Remembered Hills* (New Victoria Theatre), *The Memory of Water* (Vienna's English Speaking Theatre), *The Woman Who Swallowed a Pin* (Southwark Playhouse), *My Sister in This House* (Theatr Clwyd), *Jane Eyre* (Derby Playhouse), *Strike Gently Away From Body, Blavatsky, The Shift* and *The Art of Random Whistling* (Young Vic), *Wicked Yaar!* and *Henry V* (The National Theatre) and *Digging For Ladies* (Open Air Tour).

Film and television credits include *Alistair McGowan's Big Impression, The Inspector Lynley Mysteries, Inspector Morse, The Bill, Oranges and Lemons, Minder* and *Nietta's Film*.

Daniel Ryan Kev

Theatre credits include *Fallout* (Royal Court), *Midsummer Nights Dream, Richard III, Pericles, The Changeling, Coriolanus* and *All's Well that Ends Well* (RSC), *And This Little Piggy* (RSC Fringe), *Life After Life* (National Theatre), *Herbal Bed* (Duchess), *Viva Espana* (Arts), *The Boys from Syracuse, Macbeth* and *A Midsummer Nights Dream* (Regents Park) and *Sugar* (West Yorkshire Playhouse).

Television credits include *As Time Goes By* (DLT Productions), *The Government Inspector* (Mentorn/Channel 4), *Born and Bred* (BBC), *Steel River Blues* (Yorkshire), *Blue Murder* (Granada), *Inspector Lynley* (BBC), *The Royal* (Yorkshire), *Holby City* (BBC), *Where the Heart Is* (Anglia), *Hanging On* (Century Films/Channel 4), *Wire in the Blood* (Coastal), *2000 Acres of Sky* (Zenith/BBC), *Love or Money* (Monogram), *Bob & Rose* (Red/ITV), *Linda Green* (Red/BBC), *Throw Away the Key* (Hattrick), *Men Only* (World/C4), *Cops* (World/BBC), *City Central* (BBC), *Trial and Retribution (I & II)* (La Plante Prods), *Dangerfield* (BBC), *The Broker's Man* (Bentley Prods), *The Grove* (Carlton), *The Governor* (La Plante Prods), *Dalziel and Pascoe* (BBC), *Independent Man* (ITV), *Where the Buffalo Roam, Between the Lines, N7, Casualty* (BBC), *Seaford* (Initial), *Peak Practice* (Central), *Heartbeat, Resnick I & II* and *The Lawlord* (BBC).

Film credits include *All or Nothing, Ashes and Sand, Up on the Roof, Lipstick on your Collar, Seafood* and *Christmas Merry*.

Amelia Bullmore Writer

Amelia studied Drama at Manchester University. She started out as an actress, began writing in 1995 and continues to do both. She wrote two episodes of the second series of *This Life* for World/BBC2. She devised the series *Black Cab* for World/BBC2 and wrote three of the episodes. Amelia also wrote two episodes of the first series of *Attachments*, also for World/BBC2.

Amelia was a Dennis Potter Award Finalist in 2000 for her original 90-minute drama, *The Middle* (owned by Compulsive Viewing/BBC).

Mammals is Amelia's first play. She is currently working on a feature film for Tiger Aspect and her second stage play.

Anna Mackmin Director

Anna's credits include *Breathing Corpses* (Royal Court), *Cloud Nine* (Sheffield Crucible), *The Dark* (Donmar), *The Crucible* (Sheffield Crucible), *Food Chain* (Royal Court), *Iphigenia* (Sheffield Crucible), *Auntie & Me* (Assembly Rooms, Wyndhams, Gaiety Dublin), *Teeth 'n' Smiles* (Sheffield Crucible), *The Arbor* (Sheffield Crucible), *In Flame* (The Bush, The New Ambassadors) and *Airswimming* (BAC).

Anna was literary associate and then associate director at Sheffield Crucible with co-responsibility for programming the current season. She is also an associate director at The Gate Theatre and won the 2004 TMA award for best director for her production of *Cloud Nine*.

Alex Ferguson Assistant Director

After studying English at the University of Cambridge, Alex won the Buzz Goodbody Student Director Award (Patron: RSC) and The Bush Theatre Directing Award for his production of Enda Walsh's *Bedbound* at the National Student Drama Festival. He has studied clown and mask, and assistant directed for John Wright and Paul Burgess, as well as directing work by Endaj Walsh and Samuel Beckett, devised work and new writing. He is currently developing work with The SlungLow Collective and is working on *Lovesick*, a clown show about love and odours, for the Edinburgh Fringe.

Paul Wills Designer

Theatre credits include *Breathing Corpses* (Royal Court), *Blue/Orange* (Sheffield Crucible), *References to Salvador Dali Make Me Hot*, *Gompers* (Arcola), *Car Thieves* (Birmingham Rep), *Battina and the Moon* (Crucible Studio), *The School of Night* (The Other Place, RSC), *Young Voices* (Sheffield Theatres education tour).

As associate designer, theatre credits include *World Music* and *Grand Hotel* (Donmar), and as assistant designer for *Loyal Women* (Royal Court).

As assistant designer, other theatre credits include *Richard III*, *Don Juan*, *World Music*, *The Tempest*, *A Midsummer Night's Dream* (Crucible, Sheffield), *Privates on Parade*, *The Vortex*, *Caligula* (Donmar), *Eccentricities of a Nightingale* (Gate, Dublin), *Power* (RNT), *The Embalmer* (Almeida/tour), *Twelfth Night* (Royal Dramaten, Stockholm), *High Society*, *A Chorus Line* (Crucible, Sheffield), *Arsenic and Old Lace*, *Much Ado About Nothing*, *The Taming of the Shrew*, *The Tamer Tamed*, *All's Well That Ends Well*, *Othello* (RSC).

Howard Harrison Lighting Designer

Howard has lit productions for companies including The Royal Shakespeare Company, Royal National Theatre, Donmar Warehouse, Royal Court, Royal Opera, English National Opera, English National Ballet, Australian Opera, Kirov Opera and the Metropolitan Opera.

His current work includes *Mary Poppins* in the West End, *Mamma Mia!* on Broadway and in London, Las Vegas, Hamburg, Holland, Japan, Stockholm, Toronto, Australia and *Rebecca* on tour in the UK.

His work in the West End includes *Suddenly Last Summer* and *The Master Builder* (Albery), *Oleanna* (Garrick), *Ragtime* (Piccadilly), *The Witches Of Eastwick* (Drury Lane/Prince of Wales), *The Seven Year Itch* (Queens), *Cat On A Hot Tin Roof* and *Cyrano De Bergerac* (Lyric), *A Delicate Balance* (Theatre Royal Haymarket), *Black Comedy* (Comedy) and *Kat And The Kings* at the Vaudeville. On Broadway his work includes *Cat on a Hot Tin Roof*, *Putting It Together* and *Kat And The Kings*.

For the Donmar Warehouse, he has lit *Fool For Love*, *The Fix*, *Tales From Hollywood*, *To The Green Fields Beyond*, *Privates On Parade* and *The Vortex*.

His Opera and Dance work includes *Il Trovatore*, *Aida*, *I Masnadieri* and *Otello* (The Royal Opera), *Beatrice And Benedict* and *Cavalleria Rusticana/Pagliacci* (Welsh National Opera and Opera Australia), *Swan Lake* and *Romeo And Juliet* (English National Ballet), Matthew Bourne's *Nutcracker!* (Sadler's Wells), *Albert Herring* (Opera North), *The Elixir Of Love* (English National Opera) and *The Makropulos Case* and *Nabucco* (The Metropolitan Opera, New York).

Howard has been nominated six times as Best Lighting Designer in the Laurence Olivier Awards, and was the recipient of the 2001 Australian Green Room Award for his work on *Mamma Mia!*.

Mike Walker Sound Designer

Mike first worked at the Grand Theatre, Wolverhampton before training at The Guildhall School of Music and Drama in London.

Sound designs include *Carousel* (NT, Shaftesbury Theatre and Japan), *Oliver!* (London Palladium), *The Graduate* (London and Australia), *The Full Monty* (London and UK Tour), *Jus' Like That* (Garrick Theatre and UK Tour), *Songs My Mother Taught Me* (Savoy Theatre), *Bat Boy – The Musical* (West Yorkshire Playhouse and Shaftesbury Theatre) and *Jerry Springer – The Opera* (Edinburgh and London), for which he won the first Olivier Award for Best Sound Design. For the Bush Theatre he has designed *How Love Is Spelt*.

He was invited to Singapore in 1994 to design *Into The Woods* and has designed over twenty productions there since, including *Little Shop of Horrors*, *Sing To The Dawn*, *Hamlet*, *Art*, *They're Playing Our Song* (Singapore and Manila), *Chang & Eng* (Singapore, Bangkok and Kuala Lumpur) and *Forbidden City* which formed part of the opening festival of the *Esplanade – Theatres on The Bay*.

Mike, with his company Loh Humm Audio, provide consultancy, project management and installation services for theatres. Recent projects include work for the National Theatre, Stratford East, Albany Theatre in Deptford, Singapore Repertory Theatre and the Rose of Kingston.

The Bush Theatre

The Bush Theatre opened in April 1972 in the upstairs dining room of The Bush Hotel, Shepherds Bush Green. The room had previously served as Lionel Blair's dance studio. Since then, The Bush has become the country's leading new writing venue with over 350 productions, premiering the finest new writing talent.

"One of the most vibrant theatres in Britain, and a consistent hotbed of new writing talent." Midweek magazine

Playwrights whose works have been performed here at The Bush include:
Stephen Poliakoff, Robert Holman, Tina Brown, Snoo Wilson, John Byrne, Ron Hutchinson, Terry Johnson, Beth Henley, Kevin Elyot, Doug Lucie, Dusty Hughes, Sharman Macdonald, Billy Roche, Tony Kushner, Catherine Johnson, Philip Ridley, Richard Cameron, Jonathan Harvey, Richard Zajdlic, Naomi Wallace, David Eldridge, Conor McPherson, Joe Penhall, Helen Blakeman, Lucy Gannon, Mark O'Rowe and Charlotte Jones.

The theatre has also attracted major acting and directing talents including Bob Hoskins, Alan Rickman, Antony Sher, Stephen Rea, Frances Barber, Lindsay Duncan, Brian Cox, Kate Beckinsale, Patricia Hodge, Simon Callow, Alison Steadman, Jim Broadbent, Tim Roth, Jane Horrocks, Gwen Taylor, Mike Leigh, Mike Figgis, Mike Newell and Richard Wilson.

Victoria Wood and Julie Walters first worked together at The Bush, and Victoria wrote her first sketch on an old typewriter she found backstage.

In over 30 years, The Bush has won over one hundred awards and recently received The Peggy Ramsay Foundation Project Award 2002. Bush plays, including most recently *The Glee Club*, have transferred to the West End. Off-Broadway transfers include *Howie the Rookie* and *Resident Alien*. Film adaptations include *Beautiful Thing* and *Disco Pigs*. Bush productions have toured throughout Britain, Europe North America and Asia, most recently *Stitching, Adrenalin... Heart* (representing the UK in the Tokyo International Arts Festival, 2004) and *The Glee Club* (UK National Tour, Autumn 2004).

Every year we receive over fifteen hundred scripts through the post, and we read them all. According to The Sunday Times:

"What happens at The Bush today is at the very heart of tomorrow's theatre"

That's why we read all the scripts we receive and will continue to do so.

Mike Bradwell
Artistic Director

Fiona Clark
Executive Producer

Be There At The Beginning

The Bush Theatre is a writer's theatre – dedicated to commissioning, developing and producing exclusively new plays. Up to seven writers each year are commissioned and we offer a bespoke programme of workshops and one-to-one dramaturgy to develop their plays. Our international reputation of over thirty years is built on consistently producing the very best work to the very highest standard.

With your help this work can continue to flourish.

The Bush Theatre's Patron Scheme delivers an exciting range of opportunities for individual and corporate giving, offering a closer relationship with the theatre and a wide range of benefits from ticket offers to special events. Above all, it is an ideal way to acknowledge your support for one of the world's greatest new writing theatres.

To join, please pick up an information pack from the foyer, call 020 7602 3703 or email info@bushtheatre.co.uk

We would like to thank our current members and invite you to join them!

Rookies
Anonymous
Anonymous
David Brooks
Geraldine Caulfield
Sian Hansen
Lucy Heller
Mr G Hopkinson
Ray Miles
Malcolm & Liliane Ogden
Clare Rich & Robert
Marshall
Martin Shenfield

Beautiful Things
Anonymous
Anonymous
Alan Brodie
Kate Brooke
Clive Butler
Clyde Cooper
Patrick and Anne Foster
Vivien Goodwin
Sheila Hancock
William Keeling
Laurie Marsh
Michael McCoy
Mr & Mrs A Radcliffe
John Reynolds
Mr and Mrs George
Robinson
Tracey Scoffield
Barry Serjent
Brian D Smith

Glee Club
Anonymous
The Hon Mrs Giancarla
Alen-Buckley
Jim Broadbent
Nick Marston

Lone Star
Silver Star

Bronze Corporate Membership
Act Productions Ltd
Anonymous

Silver Corporate Membership
The Agency
Oberon Books Ltd
PFD

Platinum Corporate Membership
Anonymous

Mammals

to Paul

Characters

Jane, *thirty-five*
Kev, *thirty-nine*
Betty, *four*
Jess, *six*
Phil, *forty-one*
Lorna, *late twenties*

Scene One

A kitchen, ravaged. The floor is strewn with lidless pens, clothes and toys. Nothing looks straight or clear. **Jane** *enters, wearing pyjamas. She fills the kettle and flicks it on. With the long edge of a tray she shunts along the detritus that covers the table, leaving one end clear.* **Betty** *enters, in pyjamas.*

Betty Mum?

Jane Yes.

Betty What happens after you die?

Jane Nobody really knows. Good morning, Betty.

Betty But there is such a thing as Heaven?

Jane Lots of people believe in Heaven but nobody knows for sure.

Betty But there's no such thing as Hell.

Jane No. Hell is rubbish. What do you want for breakfast?

Betty Yasmin in Year Two believes in Hell.

Jane Well, it's absolute rubbish. Cornflakes?

Betty I DON'T KNOW YET!

Jane Don't shout. Hurry up and decide. (*Calling up to ceiling.*) Jess! We're going to be late! Come on!

Jess (*muffled, from above*) Coming!

Jane Right. What's it to be, Betty?

Betty What is there?

Jane You know what there is!

Betty DON'T SHOUT AT ME!

Jane Right. Cornflakes. (*She goes to get them.*)

Betty Stupid.

Jane Who's stupid?

Betty   CORNFLAKES ARE STUPID!

Jane   DON'T SHOUT AT ME!

Betty   WELL, DON'T SHOUT AT ME!

Jane *shakes out cornflakes, fetches a carton of milk, puts it on the table, goes to get a spoon. As she does so:*

Jane *(calling out)*   Jess, would you bring in the milk?

Jess *(offstage)*   OK!

Betty *sets about pouring her own milk.*

Jane   Hang on, Betty.

Betty   I want to do it.

Jane   No.

They both grasp the carton.

Betty   Let me do it!

Jane   Let go!

Betty   Please, Mum, I'll be careful. Please, Mum. Please.

Jane *lets go of the carton.* **Betty** *carefully tilts it.*

Jane   Two hands.

Betty *obeys. The milk pours in the smallest, slowest stream imaginable.*

Betty *(looking up with pride, her pouring hand swinging wide)*   See?

Jane *(realigning* **Betty***'s hand)*   Watch it.

Some moments pass.

Very good. You can probably go a bit quicker now.

Betty *flips the carton upside down. A gush of milk fills her bowl to the brim and empties the carton.*

Jane   Bloody hell!

Betty   YOU TOLD ME!

Jess *enters. She is dressed in school uniform, nothing done up or tucked in.*

Jess Mum. Will you give this letter to Mrs Friar? It's urgent that she gets it.

Jane Right.

Betty YOU MADE ME!

Jess I want the children who are clever as me to be given harder work.

Jane Can I see?

Jess I've licked it.

Jane Tell me what it says.

Jess I said it's boring waiting for the stupid children like Christopher and I want to learn to talk Ancient Egypt.

Jane You can't say that.

Jess Christopher knows he's stupid.

Jane You still can't say it.

Jess He doesn't mind. He's the most stupidest in the class.

Jane Where's the milk?

Jess I forgot.

Jane *exits to get the milk.* **Jess** *fetches herself a bowl and spoon. She takes neat handfuls of cornflakes out of the packet, drops them in her bowl. We hear the front door open and shut.*

Betty Jess. Jess. Mum says Hell is absolute rubbish.

Jane *re-enters, empty-handed.*

Jane Jess, you'll have to have toast.

Jess I want cornflakes.

Jane Well, you can't, there's no milk.

Jess Why's she got milk?

Jane Because she tipped it all in her bowl −

Betty I DID IT BY AN ACCIDENT −

Jane   Yes but that's what happened –

Betty   I DON'T WANT TO TALK ABOUT IT!

Jess   Bad Betty!

Jane   Jess. I tell her off, not you. It's nothing to do with you.

Jess   It is if I can't have any breakfast!

Jane   I just said you can have toast.

Jess   What if I don't want it?

Jane   Tough. What d'you want on it?

Jess   Milk.

Jane *takes a sliced loaf from the bread bin, whips out two slices, recoils, flings them and the bag into the bin.*

Jane   How about a banana?

Jess   I'm having toast.

Jane   The bread's gone mouldy.

Jess   Why did you tell me toast, then?

Jane *whips the bread out of the bin and splays the bag under* **Jess***'s nose.*

Jane   There's the bread! You want it? Have it!

Jess   Waaah! Take it away!

Betty   Let me see!

Jane *splays the bag under* **Betty***'s nose.*

Betty   Waaah!

Jane   Anybody want toast?

Betty *and* **Jess**   NO!

Jane   Right!

She flings the bread back in the bin, clangs the lid down and dumps a banana in front of **Jess***. She flicks the kettle on again, looks at her watch.*

Jane Jesus.

Jane exits. Jess gets down from the table and drops her banana in the bin. Then she hoists herself up level with the table edge so that her arms, braced straight, are supporting her. All we can see is her back view. Her hips agitate from side to side.

Betty When's Dad coming home?

Jess is too absorbed to reply. Betty eats cornflakes with her fingers. Jess continues, now emitting small sounds of exertion. And pleasure.

Betty Pretend you're dying.

Jess hops down and looks wan.

Betty Oh my darling! Are you dying?

Jess (*crumpling into Betty's arms*) Yes, I'm dying.

Betty I will give you some mentsin.

Jess Yes.

Betty It's pink mentsin.

Jess (*fading fast*) Give me some mentsin.

Betty It tastes susgusting but it works.

Jess Ah. Ahhhhhh.

Jess becomes limp.

Betty 'Oh no,' said the doctor. 'She is dead. Nuffink at all upon her face.' Let me put the mentsin in your dead mouth.

Jess hangs her mouth open. Betty spoons in imaginary medicine.

Jess I'm alive!

Betty Say, 'Alison, you're the best doctor in the world.'

Jess Alison, you're the best doctor in the world.

Betty Now you be the doctor and I'll die.

Jess I don't want to any more.

Jess resumes her rubbing. Jane re-enters, school uniform over her arm, dumps it on the sofa.

Jane   Jess.

Jess *hops down.*

Betty   When's Dad coming home?

Jane   Tonight.

Betty *and* **Jess**   Yay!

Jane   Right. Betty. 'Jamas off.

Betty *shoogles her hips about, making her pyjama trousers slide down slowly.*

Betty (*singing*)   Lalalala lalala . . .

Jane   Come on. Properly. (*She yanks the pyjama trousers off.*) Knicks.

Betty *steps into her pants.*

Betty (*singing*)   Her pants were pink. And she was beautiful.

While **Jane** *is occupied,* **Jess** *resumes rubbing.* **Jane** *begins to bunch up one leg of a pair of grey tights. She kneels at* **Betty**'s *feet.*

Jane   Foot.

Betty *dangles the wrong foot.*

Jane   Other foot.

Betty *dangles other foot.*

Betty   I'm going to tell Yasmin in Year Two that Hell is rubbish. (*She sees her tights for the first time.*) These are not beautiful!

Jane   They're school tights.

Betty   I'm not wearing them!

Jane   You are.

Betty   Take them off!

Jane   No. Come on. You wear these every day.

Jane *dips to pick up* **Betty**'s *school skirt.* **Betty** *makes a dash for it.* **Jane** *grabs her roughly by the arm.* **Betty** *strains away.*

Jane   Oy! Where you going?

Betty   TOILET!

Jane   I don't believe you. Get your skirt on.

Betty   DO YOU WANT ME TO POO IN MY PANTS?

They eyeball each other. **Betty** *snatches the skirt and runs off.*

Jane   Hurry up!

She turns to **Jess**.

Jane   Jess!

Jess *continues.*

Jane   *Come on!* We're going to be late.

Jess *hops down.* **Jane** *does up* **Jess**'s *buttons, tucks in her clothes as:*

Jess   You've got a hairy fanny.

Jane   I have.

Jess   Will I get one?

Jane   When you're big.

Jess   I don't want one.

Jane   Why?

Jess   It looks disgusting.

Jane   I don't think it does.

Jess   It does.

Betty *re-enters. She has put on her skirt, but removed her grey tights and replaced them with pink socks.*

Jane   You are *unbelievable*! Go and get your tights!

Betty   No!

Jane   Do as you're told!

Betty   You don't love me any more!

Jane GO!

Betty *runs off, snivelling.* **Jess** *fastens her shoes.* **Jane** *combs hair out of the hairbrush and lifts the lid of the bin to chuck it. She seizes the banana.*

Jane What's this?

Jess I didn't want it.

Jane You can't just put it in the bin!

Jess I never said I wanted it!

Jane Doesn't mean you can waste it!

Jess Well, if you gave me proper breakfast I wouldn't have to throw it away!

Jane You didn't have to!

Jess You're supposed to feed children. You're supposed to go to shops and buy us food we like!

Jane You like bananas!

Jess I don't.

Jane You've just decided you don't, but you do.

Jess All right then, make me eat it! Make me eat something I hate!

Jane Calm down.

Jess Give me the banana!

Jane No.

Jess Now you won't give me something to eat!

Jane (*very calm*) Do you really want this?

Jess Yes!

Jane Calm down. Listen to me. Are you going to eat it?

Jess Yes.

Jane *unpeels the banana and gives it to* **Jess.** **Jess** *takes a bite. A moment. She spits it out into her hand.*

Jess It's mashy.

Jane, *face like thunder, takes the banana, drops it in the bin, replaces the lid and turns her back on* **Jess**. **Betty** *shuffles in, the grey tights round her ankles, pleased with what this does to her walk.*

Betty Look!

With grim speed, **Jane** *yanks up the tights and·dresses* **Betty**.

Betty Ow! Ouch! You're hurting me!

Jane Don't care.

Betty Ow!

Jane Shut up.

Jess Stop hurting my sister!

Jane *swings for* **Jess** *and whacks her.*

Jane Don't you *dare* tell me what to do!

Jess *reels back, shocked and winded.* **Betty** *is transfixed.*

Jane You push it and you push it and you push it!

Slowly, **Jess** *pulls up her shirt to reveal reddened skin.*

Jess Look.

Jane *looks.*

Jane We've got to go.

Betty I need a cuddle.

Jane Coats on.

Betty I need a cuddle now!

Jane *holds* **Betty**.

Jane Now go and get your coat on.

Betty *runs off.*

Jess Are you sorry?

Jane No.

Jess I hate you.

Jane *wipes her hands over her face.*

Jane Jess. If you tell Dad about this he will be very cross and upset with us.

Jess You hit me!

Jane It wasn't hard.

Jess You nearly killed me!

Jane It was just a bit of a thump. But it would really upset Dad if he knew you made me so cross that it happened. Shall I tell him?

Jess No!

Jane OK, let's not tell him. Good girl. Come on.

Jane *exits.* **Jess** *hops up and rubs.*

Jane (*offstage*) Where's your book bag?

Betty (*offstage*) I don't know!

Jane (*offstage*) There it is. Pick it up.

Betty (*offstage*) Stop telling me what to do!

Jane (*offstage*) Jess! Now!

Jess *hops down and exits kitchen. Sound of front door being opened.*

Jane (*offstage*) Coat! Out! OUT!

Front door slams shut.

Blackout.

Scene Two

Lights up. Sound of front door opening and shutting. **Jane** *enters. She wears a long coat and boots. She clicks the kettle on. She slips off her coat. She is still in her pyjamas, which are tucked into the boots. She picks up some dishes from the table. She puts them down. She sits on the floor. She replaces the lid of one pen. She lies down, defeated.*

Sound of key in front door. She starts.

Jane (*alarmed, standing*)   Hello?

She listens to footsteps approaching. **Kev** *enters.* **Jane** *is amazed.*

Kev   Good togs.

Jane (*delighted*)   What's going on?

She wraps herself around him. He holds her. They moan a duet of reunion sounds. He goes to kiss her. She ducks.

I haven't brushed my teeth.

Kev   I don't care.

Jane   How come you're so early?

Kev   I begged.

Jane   It's a shit-hole. Sorry.

Kev   It's fine.

He looks at the mess, which depresses him greatly.

Jane   You look young.

Kev   Do I?

Jane   Round the eyes.

Kev   You've got sleep in yours.

With his finger he clears the sleep away. She holds her face unblinkingly for him to do this as:

This hasn't been done since last time I was home.

Jane   That's why you have to come back every week. Stop me crusting over.

Kev   There.

Jane   I love you.

He kisses her.

Kev   How are the girls?

Jane   Foul. But not as foul as me.

Kev   It's hard.

Jane   It's all right when you're here.

Kev   Well, when I'm here you don't have to do it all, so you've got more patience.

Jane   I've started inviting their friends round just so I'll behave better. Are you all right?

Kev   Are you?

Jane   Fine.

She kisses him and moves away to fold laundry. He joins her.

Mum phoned.

Kev   Yeah?

Jane   Clare's been promoted.

Kev   Wow.

Jane   Maggie's gone to Bhutan for a month.

Kev   Wow.

Jane   What do you think they say about me? 'My sister cooked some pasta. And she served it with sauce, from a jar, and grated cheese. She's astounding.'

Jane *throws one end of a sheet to him. He catches it. They fold it in half long-ways. They get it wrong, so there's a twist. They put it right. They walk towards each other to make their ends meet. As she takes it from him into her pinched fingers he covers her hands with his and won't let go. He drops his head.*

Kev   Oh Jane.

Jane   What?

Kev   I'm in a mess.

Jane   Tell me.

He doesn't raise his head. She eases the sheet from his fingers, folds the last fold and slings it over a chair.

Tell me.

Kev   I think I'm in love with someone.

Jane   No.

Kev   I'm sorry.

Jane   No.

Kev   We always said if we ever got in trouble, we'd tell. So I am. I'm so sorry. Nothing's happened.

She stares at him a moment.

Jane   Who has nothing happened with?

Kev   I love you.

Jane   Is it Adjoa?

Kev   No.

Jane   Phillippa?

Kev   No, it's Fay.

Jane   I like Fay.

Kev   She likes you. I'm so sorry.

Jane   You're in love with Fay?

Kev   I don't know what it is, but I didn't want it. Maybe it's just a crush. I don't know.

Jane   Is she in love with you?

Kev   I've no idea.

Jane   Have you told her you're in love with her?

Kev   No! No.

Jane   You're supposed to love me.

Kev   I do! That's what I don't understand. This doesn't rob from loving you. It doesn't come from the same . . . supply.

She stares at him, stricken.

I had to tell you.

Jane   What am I supposed to do with it?

Kev I don't know.

Jane What are you going to do?

Kev Nothing.

Jane Is she still with that Geordie guy?

Kev No. He treated her very badly.

She stares at him a moment.

Jane How much longer is she on the team?

Kev Till the summer. If we finish on time. Nothing's going to happen. It's going to be fine.

Jane Says who?

Kev Because it's not telling that's dangerous. You're my wife. You're my Jane. I tell you things.

Jane I don't know what it is you're telling me. Are you – is it – do you just . . . fancy her? Or are you in love with her? Or what?

Kev I have – irrational feelings for her.

Jane Such as what?

Kev I can't describe it.

Jane D'you think about her all the time?

Kev I do think about her.

Jane A lot?

Kev Yes.

Jane How d'you feel when you're with her?

Kev Good.

Terrified, she's waiting for more.

Excited.

And more.

I feel very . . . myself.

Jane   D'you want to leave me?

Kev   No. Emphatically no.

She stares at him, blowing her nose. She perches her bum on the table.

Jane   You've got to fuck me.

Kev   Have I?

Jane   Immediately.

He goes to her. She rubs his cock. Undoes his fly. They kiss.

Come on. You're ready. I'm ready. Come on.

Kev   I love you, Jane.

Jane   Come on!

They get one of her pyjama legs off over her boot.

Kev   I don't want to. Sorry.

Jane *is speechless with hurt. She struggles her boot back into her pyjama leg. He goes to help. She snatches herself away from him.*

Jane   You've never done that before.

Kev   I'd rather talk.

Jane   You don't want me.

Kev   No, I just don't want sex, now.

Jane   You say you love me but you won't touch me.

Kev   That's not – that's – that's – over-simple.

Jane   I feel like a leper.

Kev   OK. Let's start again. Let's do it. Come on.

Jane   (*incredulous outrage*)   NO!

The doorbell rings.

Kev   You expecting anyone?

Jane   No.

The letterbox flap clatters open.

Phil (*offstage*) Jane! Halloo! You there?

Kev and **Jane** *are amazed.*

Kev Sounds like Phil.

Jane They're not due till tonight.

Kev I didn't know they were coming.

Jane It was a surprise.

Kev (*calling to front door*) Just a minute! (*He does up his fly.*) I do love you.

He exits. **Jane** *straightens up as we hear the front door opening.*

Phil (*offstage*) I didn't think you'd be here till tonight!

Kev (*offstage*) Snap!

Phil (*offstage*) You know what I did? We decided last minute to drive through the night and beat the traffic and I thought Jane won't mind, I'll phone up and warn her first thing, she'll be up with the girls – and I've got this brand new phone, which is so beautiful and tiny it's practically *Fabergé* – and I'm so chuffed with it and I wanted to show it off to you but – I'm such an *arse* – I forgot to put your number in it.

Phil *enters kitchen.*

Phil Hello, my darling. In her pyjamas! Oh God, were you having a lovely lazy morning which we've just ruined?

Jane Yes. Hello.

They embrace very fondly as **Kev** *enters, carrying a carton of milk.*

Jane You smell nice, what's that?

Phil Tesco Economy Laundry Liquid.

Kev (*looking back, confused, at the still open front door*) Is Lorna coming?

Phil Yes. She's just improving my parking.

Kev Right. Milk's arrived.

Jane Good. Tea? Coffee? Water?

Phil   Heroin.

Jane *laughs.*

Phil   Tea.

Jane *goes to kettle.*

How are you?

Kev   Fine. You?

Phil   Fine.

Kev   Good.

Catch-up complete, they smile at each other. Very fond. **Phil** *has a puff on his inhaler.*

Phil   I must pee. Oh God, I must pee.

Phil *exits.*

Kev   You OK?

Jane   No.

Kev   We'll talk later.

Jane   I don't want to talk. I don't want to look at you. I don't want to be here.

Lorna (*offstage*)   Hi!

Jane   Hi!

Jane *exits to meet* **Lorna**. **Kev** *assumes kettle duty.*

Jane (*offstage*)   Good to see you.

Lorna (*offstage*)   And you.

Jane (*offstage*)   Are there any other bags?

Lorna   No, that's it.

The women enter the kitchen. **Lorna** *is tall and has great style.*

Lorna   Hiya, Kev.

Kev   Hello there.

He kisses her.

You look very well.

Jane   You do. You look great.

Lorna   I stink, unfortunately.

Jane   Long journey.

Lorna   Mmmm.

Kev   Phil's having a tea. D'you fancy one?

Lorna   No. Just water, please.

Kev   Comin' up.

Jane   Sorry the place is such a tip.

Lorna   We're nine hours early, you're entitled to be in another continent.

Jane *clears up in a hurried, inefficient way.* **Lorna** *watches.*

Lorna   Where are the girls?

Jane   School.

Lorna (*amazed*)   Betty's at school?

Jane   Yeah. Just started.

Kev *hands her her water.*

Lorna   Thanks.

Lorna *takes cigarettes from her bag and heads for the door to the yard.*

Kev   Have it in here.

Lorna   The yard's fine.

Kev   There's no need.

Lorna   I always smoke in your yard.

Kev   Well, if it's love of tradition, go ahead, but don't –

Lorna   It is. I'm not taking you into account in any way.

Kev Good.

Lorna *sweeps out.* **Kev** *joins* **Jane** *clearing up in silence. After some moments* **Jane** *hits* **Kev** *very hard. He spins round, astonished.* **Phil** *enters.*

Phil Much better.

Kev *holds himself where he was hit.*

Phil You OK?

Kev Fine. Nasty cold cup of tea for you over there.

Phil Super.

Silence as **Phil** *drinks tea.*

Jane So how was the drive?

Phil Oh, you know. I haven't enjoyed driving to or from Scotland since I was about eighteen. Actually I never recovered from the disappointment of Scotch Corner, which I thought was going to be a brake-screeching right-angle hung with tartan.

Jane *smiles.*

Phil Have I said that before?

Jane I still like it.

Phil *peers out of the window which gives on to the yard.*

Phil Where's your buddleia?

Jane Had to chop it down.

Phil Why?

Jane It was growing out of the wall.

Phil It was a great big tree!

Jane I know. It'd seeded itself. The wall was about to fall down.

Phil What a shame. It always looked so great in the summer.

Jane   I know, and Jess loved it 'cause she could look down from her bedroom and see butterflies.

Phil   So did you fell a big tree all by yourself, Kev?

Kev   I did.

Phil   Very good.

Lorna re-enters and drops her cigarette end in the kitchen bin.

Jane   I poisoned the stump. You have to, otherwise it keeps growing back. I had to paint it with this stuff called – oh, not KGB. What was it? SBK! Synthetic Brushwood Killer.

Phil   Whereas the KGB – Kills Genuine Brushwood.

Jane   Was that prepared?

Phil   No!

Jane   No one's that quick.

Phil   How often d'you think Synthetic Brushwood Killer crops up?

Jane   How can he be so quick?

Lorna shrugs, underwhelmed.

Phil   You girls just have to accept that I'm a – genuinely – unusually funny, quick-witted guy.

Jane *laughs and looks to* **Lorna** *for an eye-roll.* **Lorna** *is poker-faced.*

Phil   Did you lock up the van, darlin'?

Lorna shakes her head, 'No,' and chucks him the keys. **Phil** *exits.*

Lorna   I'm not speaking to him.

Jane   Why?

Lorna   Huge fight in the car.

Jane   What about?

Lorna   Too boring to tell. That's why I stink. Why does arguing make you smell?

Jane   Driving lessons do, too.

Kev   And drilling.

Lorna   Really?

Kev   It's the fear of drilling into pipes and cables, I think. Makes me sweat like a pig. I do DIY in my knickers now.

Phil *re-enters.*

Phil   Does anyone want anything from the offie?

Kev   It's ten o'clock!

Phil   For later. Some wine for dinner.

Kev   I've got some.

Phil   Some decent wine.

Kev *smiles.* **Lorna** *glares at* **Phil**.

Phil   Anybody?

Jane   No thanks.

Phil   Lorna?

Lorna *shakes her head.*

Phil   Are you all right for cigarettes?

Lorna *nods.*

Phil   Would you like to come for the ride?

Lorna   No. I'd like to have a bath.

Jane   There's plenty of hot water.

Lorna   Great.

Lorna *picks up her bag.*

Kev   Do you know where you're going? We've moved all the rooms round to confuse guests. Here.

He takes her weekend bag. **Lorna** *follows him.* **Phil** *loiters.*

Phil   We had a huge fight in the car.

Jane   She said. What about?

Phil   We only have one fight. It comes in many different guises but the basic argument is: are we or are we not a couple? Are we riding a tandem or are we two unicyclists in a head-to-head?

Jane   Of course you're a couple.

Phil   We're not. We're a three-year-long one-night stand. We're fine. I think she thinks I want to own her, but I don't. I'm honoured to have her on loan.

Jane *smiles.*

Phil   I'm still intrigued by the bottle bank.

Jane   Oh. Forget it.

Phil   What happened?

Jane   Nothing. I just. Had a feeling. I felt mad. So I phoned, as you know, and by the time you phoned back, it'd passed, so –

Phil   No, don't get slidey on me. I won't have it. If I'd picked up the phone you would have told me on the spot, so it's my due to find out what happened to you at the bottle bank and you will duly tell me.

She weighs up whether or not she should tell him.

Jane   I was shoving the bottles in – you know there's a hole you push the bottles through – sort of brushy –

Phil   – like a great bristly arsehole –

Jane   Yes. And I was really banging them through with all my strength and my teeth were gritted and I was just ramming them in to make as much of a smash as I could. And I wished I had more bottles so I could keep on smashing. And then I started thinking about all the broken glass inside the bottle bank. And the cutting it could do. And I stopped wanting to chuck in bottles and I started to want to chuck in – flesh. I wanted to drop someone naked in – from high up – onto the spikes of glass. I was . . . taken over by wanting to hurt someone. That's what happened to me at the bottle bank.

Phil   Who do you want to hurt?

Jane   I don't know.

Phil   This is the brain of a mother taking a break. You spend all your time looking after people, don't you? So from time to time you have to fantasise about violent death.

Jane   Do I?

Phil   You don't want to drop yourself onto spikes of glass, do you?

Jane   I don't think so.

Phil   Some people have that cutting thing. They cut themselves and feel better. That's not something you . . . is it?

Jane   No. I cut myself in a dream the other night.

Phil   Did you?

Jane   I was cutting up carrot sticks for the girls. And I was chopping away and the knife slipped and it cut my finger in two, and inside my finger was snakes. It didn't hurt and there was no blood and I just thought, 'Oh that's interesting; I'm made of snakes.'

Phil   Snakes are sex, aren't they? Snakes are cocks.

Jane   No, it's an anxiety dream about being a bad person. Being made of snakes.

Phil   It's a dream about being made of cocks.

Jane *laughs.*

Phil   Jane, I want you to be honest with me. I'm your husband's best friend. Are you made of cocks?

Jane (*laughing*)   No.

Phil   Come on. My name is Jane and I'm made of cocks.

She's crying.

What's this?

Jane   Kev's in love.

Phil's *astounded.*

Phil   Who with?

Jane   A woman he works with called Fay.

Phil   I think I met her once.

Jane   I've met her a lot.

Phil   Well, that's who you want to drop into a bottle bank.

Jane   No, I only just found out. Kev came home early to tell me.

Phil   What did he say?

Jane   He said; 'Nothing's happened and everything's going to be all right.'

Phil   What else did he say?

Jane   We didn't have very long, because –

Phil   – we arrived. Oh God. We'll go.

Jane   Please don't.

Phil   We must.

Jane   No, stay. Please. The worst thing he said – he said Fay's ex had treated her very badly. He said it in a protective way. Like it was a scandal. Like he would never treat her badly. He's in love with her.

Phil   He's telling you though, that's good.

Jane   Has he told you?

Phil   Not a word.

Jane   He says he hasn't told her.

Phil   Do you think it's true?

Jane   I can't tell.

Phil   What's he playing at?

Jane   I think this is how you lose people.

Phil   It's a blip.

Jane   What if it's a slow puncture?

Phil   It won't be.

Jane   Tell me what to do.

Phil (*after some time*)   Have you told him about me?

Jane   No.

Phil   Don't you think it's germane?

Lorna (*offstage*)   Jane?

Jane   Yes!

Lorna (*offstage*)   Could I borrow some salt?

Jane   Yes! You think I should tell him?

Lorna *enters, partly undressed for her bath.*

Lorna   My dentist says I've got to gargle with salt water. For my gums.

Jane (*to* **Phil**)   Do you?

Phil   I just wondered.

Jane   What's wrong with your gums?

Lorna   They're fine now, but my mum ended up with a donkey gob so I'm taking precautions.

Jane *gives her salt.*

Lorna   Ta.

Jane   D'you know where Kev is?

Lorna   Locked in the bog.

Jane   I'm going to put some clothes on.

Jane *slips away. With some distaste,* **Lorna** *navigates the sink clutter to prepare her gargle.* **Phil** *picks up his car keys and* **Kev**'s *door keys.* **Lorna** *spins round, angry.*

Lorna   What is it with you? Hours battling it out in the van and then you get here and announce you're going to buy some wine for *dinner!* I told you! I don't want to have dinner here. We agreed. We're in London. I want to feel like I'm in London. I don't want to be stuck in wheely-bin land, I want to go out! I want to eat Korean, I want to ride in a rickshaw –

Phil   – for that authentic London experience –

Lorna   Oh fuck off, you know what I mean. We're here this afternoon, we're here for lunch tomorrow –

Phil   We're not here for dinner tonight, OK, so shut up.

Lorna   We're going out?

Phil   Yes.

Lorna   They don't mind?

Phil   They need to talk. Kev's in love with someone else.

Lorna   Fuck. What's the story?

Phil   Woman called Fay. Nothing's happened yet.

He makes to go.

Lorna   Where you going?

Phil   Offie.

Lorna   Why?

Phil   I can't not buy them wine just because we're not going to drink it!

Lorna   Why not?

Phil   Do you think the road rolls up after you've driven along it?

Lorna   You're such a bitch. Your friends think you're a lovely guy, you know.

Phil   They treat me like one. They expect me to be one. That's the difference.

He starts to go.

Lorna   Phil.

Phil   What?

Lorna   I need more ciggies.

Phil   Fine.

He starts to go again.

Lorna   You are a lovely guy and I do sometimes treat you well. I treated you magnificently just before we left, didn't I?

Phil   You did.

Lorna   We go to sweet and dark and dirty places, don't we?

Phil   We do.

Lorna   And we have a laugh.

Phil   We do.

Lorna   You know the cosy weekendy thing's not my cup of tea.

Phil   I think cosy's off the menu.

Lorna   So don't take me places where you know I'll rebel.

Phil   Where does that leave? Goodbye.

Lorna   Bye, darlin'.

They kiss. He goes. **Lorna** *gargles.* **Jane** *enters, dressed.* **Jane** *picks up one of the half-completed domestic tasks.* **Lorna** *spits.*

Lorna   Seen this? It's our latest model.

Lorna *picks up her handbag, a very desirable and beautiful thing.* **Jane** *handles it reverently.*

Jane   It's gorgeous.

Lorna   We always line with cerise leather. It's the GAFFNEY CRIPPS trade mark.

Jane   How amazing. To have your own business, with your name on things.

Lorna   It is. I love it. Sometimes I lurk near the counter in Jenner's and wait to see if anyone'll buy one. And once I heard this woman going on and on, stroking the leather and crooning about how much she *loved* GAFFNEY CRIPPS and I wanted to jump up and down and shout 'That's me! I made that!' I didn't.

Jane   I wish I was arty.

Lorna   I made myself arty. The most interesting people at school were, so I converted myself from maths person to art person. I willed myself. No talent.

Jane   You must've.

Lorna   No. Now Phil is talented. Amazing drawer, amazing graphic eye, amazing at colour – but he's missing the ambition gene. I just knew what I wanted.

Jane   Well, you got it.

Lorna   Nearly. I need to shed the CRIPPS bit and break London.

Jane   I thought you liked her!

Lorna   Oh I do, but I don't want to be in partnership. I want it to be just me.

Jane   Wouldn't you be scared?

Lorna   Of me? No. You know about my plan to steal my granny back?

Jane   No.

Lorna   Well, my mum's shacked up with this sunburnt git in Spain and she's moved my granny over there. My granny doesn't like it and she's having a horrible time. So, as soon as I've made enough money I'm going to buy a big house, split it into two flats, steal my granny back from Spain, move her into her own little flat and pay her an allowance from the profits of GAFFNEY bags.

Jane   Just like that.

Lorna   Why not?

Jane   You're extraordinary.

Lorna   I just shoot my mouth off.

Pause.

What's she like?

Jane   Who?

Lorna   Fay.

Jane *looks at* **Lorna**, *incredulous.*

Lorna   Why not? I'm not your husband. I'm not your husband's best friend. But I'm stuck in your house and I'm female. Do you know her?

Jane *nods.*

Lorna   So tell me.

Pause.

Jane   She's – I don't know her well. She's . . .

Lorna   Thin? Fat?

Jane   Neither. Normal. Nice.

Lorna   Sexy?

Jane   Look. No. Come on. This is – glib.

Lorna   Got to start somewhere.

Pause.

Jane   Well, I wouldn't have said so, no, but since this morning I'm beginning to think she must be sexy –

Lorna   – otherwise he wouldn't want to fuck her.

Jane   Yes. Which makes me think maybe it's not the ones who look like a threat who actually are. Maybe I just can't see it, 'cause I'm not a man.

Lorna   Women always think I'm a threat.

Jane   But you're not.

Lorna   No, I am – it's a double-bluff thing with me. But he hasn't fucked her?

Jane   No. He hasn't. Nothing's happened.

Lorna   So his crime is he fancies her?

Jane   He said 'in love'.

Lorna   You must have fancied people since you've been with Kev.

Jane   I haven't actually.

Lorna   Never?

Jane   Stop. Stop grilling me. I've told you enough.

Lorna   You've told me nothing. Nothing big. Nothing dangerous. Nothing that'll change anything. You could have told me anything and I'd never have said a word. People never tell the big things. I don't love Phil.

Jane   What?

Lorna   That would be a big thing to tell.

Jane   It's not true though, is it?

Lorna   I'm waiting for someone I still love, and who used to love me, to come back. And when he does, I'll leave Phil. That would also be a big thing to tell.

Jane   What are you up to?

Lorna   The man I'm waiting for picked me up and put me down and picked me up and put me down for three years till I didn't know what my name was. I lived on apples for a year. I had to sleep with a pillow between my knees if I lay on my side because my own bones kept me awake. We finished five years ago. I don't know where he is. Amsterdam's the last I heard. I look for him everywhere I go. I've scanned every station platform, every bus stop, every cinema queue, every garage forecourt – anywhere peopled – for five years. What I've been *doing* is making bags, setting up the business,

looking like I'm living – but what I've really been doing is
waiting for him. And if he comes for me, I'll go. Not for the
pain. I've no interest in pain. What I'm after is the end of
the story.

Jane *stares, bemused, at* **Lorna**.

Lorna   Now just imagine if I told you that! That would be
huge!

Jane   If you don't love Phil, you shouldn't be messing about
with him.

Lorna   What I feel for Phil – most people, if they felt it,
would stand up in court and swear it was love! It's what's
come to be known as love. Rubbing along, having a laugh,
having enough of the kind of sex you like, liking them
enough to put up with the terrible things they do because
they're not you. That's what we call love. And all the
millions of people who feel that, thank their lucky stars
they're in the love room and not outside it, cold and lonely.
But the love room's a con. The love room is actually just a
holding space. But the very very lucky few, casually leaning
on a wall in the love room, occasionally, accidentally open a
hidden door and fall through to the *real* love room. Which is
smaller and emptier and totally beautiful. I've been there.
But not with Phil.

Jane   With the man you're waiting for?

Lorna   Oh, he'll never come, Jane. I'm such a silly girl.

Jane (*increasingly flinty*)   So there's standard love, but those of
us who feel it – and we think we're doing OK – haven't
noticed it's standard. And then there's de luxe love –
enjoyed by a tiny few, including you. Is that it?

Lorna   I'm lucky.

Jane   How do you know all the people you think are just
rubbing along aren't scaling the heights like you?

Lorna   I just do.

Jane   What's your point?

Lorna   I understand why people don't tell. I never do. Things lose their power when you tell.

Jane   So was that all bullshit?

Lorna   Most of it.

Jane   Which bits?

Kev *enters.*

Lorna   Hiya.

Nobody says anything for ages.

Have I seen you since we went to Cuba?

Kev   No.

Lorna   It was fabulous. I want to go to Russia next. I want to go on the Trans-Siberian railway all the way to Beijing. I want to see Lake Baikal. It's the deepest lake in the world. It's in Siberia. There's this fish that lives about a kilometre down and it's just a sort of pink jelly with a spine and enormous eyes. And when you bring it to the top it dissolves into a spot of oil.

Kev   Why do people bring it to the top?

Lorna *shrugs.*

Lorna   You going anywhere this year?

Kev   We're talking about Devon.

Lorna *laughs.*

Lorna   Sorry.

Kev   It's funny.

Lorna   Right. Bath time.

She exits.

Kev   Hello, sweetheart.

Jane   Hello.

Kev   I've been waiting for you in the bedroom.

Jane Lorna needed some salt. And before that I was talking to Phil.

Kev Did you tell him about Fay?

Jane Yes.

Kev Don't talk to him. Talk to me. We'll sort it out.

Jane We don't go anywhere, do we?

Kev We will. Jane, please can we talk?

Jane No. I want to go for a walk.

Kev Please don't shut me out. We need to talk.

Jane Well, I need to think first, then we'll talk.

Kev When?

Jane Tonight. That girl is a fucking nut. (*She slips on her coat.*) I'll get the girls from school on my way back.

He nods. She takes her coat and exits. Sound of front door opening and closing. Some moments pass. **Kev** *goes to his jacket. He takes out his phone. He checks for a message. There isn't one. He punches a number from the phone's memory.*

Kev (*striving for a light touch*) Hello, Fay. Just ringing to say. I hope the presentation goes well. I'm sure it will. I hope you're OK. I'm home. I'm fine. I hope you are. Well. That's it. See you Monday. Have a good weekend. Bye. It's Kev. Bye.

Sound of front door opening. **Kev** *puts his phone away. Footsteps approach.* **Phil** *enters, carrying a cardboard box with six bottles of wine in it.* **Kev**'*s door keys hang from his mouth.* **Kev** *removes the keys.* **Phil** *puts down the wine.*

Phil Get stuck in.

Kev Thank you very much.

Kev *puts the wine out of the way.*

Phil Kev, what's this about Fay?

Kev   It's true. It's terrible. I'm in love.

Phil   Why didn't you tell me?

Kev   Because I was trying not to be. Sorry. It's not to do with Jane.

Phil   What d'you think it is to do with?

Kev   Fay.

Phil   I met her. When I dropped your suit off.

Kev   That's right. God. If you'd said to me then, 'You'll be crazy about this woman in six month's time,' I'd've said, 'Out of the question.' I can picture that Fay, but she seems completely different from this Fay. That Fay had no effect on me. Weird.

Phil   So what d'you think's happened in that six months?

Kev   What d'you mean?

Phil   You know – any external thing that might have fuelled it?

Kev *looks at him.*

Phil   You've been away from home a lot.

Kev   This isn't about that. This is not one of those. This is about being bothered to the roots by the idea of someone.

Phil   I wasn't trying to undermine.

Kev   I'm stuck in something which sounds like a cliché, but it's very specific to me. And very real.

Phil   Fine. OK.

Silence.

Kev   Could I just tell you? Without consequence?

Phil   Yeah.

Kev   Well. Fay lived with this Geordie guy for years and she was always rushing home to him. Or you'd hear her phoning him in a panic to say she'd be late back or whatever – you could tell she was sort of smoothing his feathers all the time – so she was only ever sort of half-present at work. Nice. Bright. Quite cute but – elsewhere. They split up around Christmas and he started stalking her like a jealous maniac and we all thought she'd go trotting back but she didn't. And then the Plymouth contract came up and she thought, 'Great. Fate,' and she just threw herself into it. She's really brave. She's sort of shed a skin. She's got a spark to her. The Big Cheese at Plymouth's an idiot, but she's got this way with him. She manages to be disrespectful and butter him up at the same time. And win the argument. And she only comes up to here on him. God, it's good to say this! I haven't been able to tell anybody any of this. Anyway, sometimes me and Fay ended up on the same train to Plymouth, but we both had work so we hardly talked. And then we ditched the train 'cause we needed cars the other end to drive to and from the site. And then hers needed a service one week so I gave her a lift. Four-and-a-half-hour car journey and we talked non-stop. It poured out of us. I can't remember half of what we said, but we laughed a lot. She's got a gorgeous laugh. Gorgeous smile. Little blunt teeth like a kid. And then just outside Plymouth, on the A386, she fell asleep. And I felt incredibly happy, painfully happy, that she was in my charge or something, or that she trusted me or something. I don't know. And that was the end of sanity.

He looks shyly at **Phil***, but his eyes are bright and there is an irrepressible vitality about him.*

Phil   And how was it for Fay? A kip in a car or a *coup de foudre*?

Kev   I didn't ask.

Phil   Have you told her how you feel?

Kev   No.

Phil   That's good.

Kev   (*energised*)   We're just mammals at the mercy of urges! You know, whatever the drugs are, the hormones – the dopamines and the endorphins and the seratonin – they're fucking pumping round my body. I think the red and white cells got booted out weeks ago – no room. My mouth tastes different! My jeans are loose!

Phil Yeah, the chemical thing can be – ferocious.

Kev Don't tell me you can do that on your own. It wouldn't make evolutionary sense to have that kind of response to someone if you left them completely cold, would it?

Phil I just don't know.

Kev I love Jane. And also, at the same time, this is happening.

Phil *nods, watching* **Kev**, *who is becoming increasingly animated.*

Kev I've been thinking about blokes who say, you know, 'Married forty years, never looked at another woman,' and it's a damning admission. It's like saying, I grew a skin over my heart – I stopped it being receptive – so I could stay faithful to my wife. Your wife's got fidelity from a dead heart. That's worth nothing. I like my heart how it is but it's – it's disobedient.

Phil *looks worried.*

Kev What?

Phil Yes, we're mammals. And hormones and urges, of course, yeah, all of that. But one of the perks of being a human type of mammal is consciousness. A conscious brain that hopefully can have a meaningful flow of dialogue with heart, and – you're looking pissed off.

Kev (*pissed off*) No, no.

Phil Well, yes, the heart is disobedient, but you can kick it into touch. The brain can show it who's boss. (*He has a puff on his inhaler.*) You say this has nothing to do with Jane. If you tell Fay you're in love with her – if the Fay thing makes any progress of any kind – it will have everything to do with Jane.

Silence.

Kev   *Conflicting* things are happening to me. Polarised but parallel forces are pulling on me. It's intricate. It's useless just telling me to be a good boy.

Phil   I'm not.

Kev   You are.

Phil   Well, maybe it's out of my league.

A shrug from **Kev**.

Phil   Oh, you think it is!

Kev   I didn't say it.

Phil   But you don't disagree.

Kev   You're not married. It's not controversial to say that, is it?

Phil   Of course not.

Kev   Right. Well, that's all I mean.

Phil   I know about women.

Kev   You haven't loved the same one for twelve years. Or been married. It's different. It just is.

Phil   I've lived with women.

Kev   Just till they go.

Phil   That's not my fault!

Kev   You pick the ones who'll go. I don't think I ever saw Kathleen with her coat off. That's fine. It suits you.

Phil   How do you know?

Kev   You told me!

Phil   When?

Kev   Here. In this kitchen. Two years ago. Three years ago.

Phil   Well, I don't remember that.

Kev   You definitely said it.

Phil   Well, it's no longer the case.

Kev Fair enough.

Phil I lived with Gina for two years! I lived with Rachelle for –

Kev I'm not saying you don't know about hair in the plughole and blood on the bog seat, the moods and the mystery –

Phil I do!

Kev I know, I'm saying you do! Everyone does. That's the cartoon of it – that's the cartoon of living with a woman.

Phil What don't I know, then?

Kev I don't want to get into this.

Phil I do. What are you saying?

Kev I'm saying, yes, this is what I'm saying. I'm saying I don't think you've ever stuck around once the surprises have run out.

Phil Two years with Gina was hardly a non-stop gasp of amazement.

Kev Discovering goes on a long time. Oh, you're a Buildings Safety Inspector! What's *that*? Oh you have a sweet little bumcrack that bends round to the left! Oh, you didn't go on a plane till you were twenty! That can go on for two, three years, easy. You can keep recruiting over and over again based on the same charming past life. If you stick with the same person, the rate of surprises drops to next to nothing. You might amaze each other twice a year. It can feel like the tide's gone out. That's proper. What you know about them, and everything they know about you. And then you have to do new things, now, that are surprising.

Phil Like fall in love with someone else.

Kev Fuck off.

Phil So tell me. Open my eyes to the real world of women. Unseal the secret casket of marriage – what happens after the tide's gone out?

Kev It comes back in.

Phil So wait patiently at the water's edge and stop fucking about in the sand dunes! Don't confuse having a dishwasher with being a man of substance. I may have had a series of love affairs with an array of tremendous women instead of hitching my wagon to one, but I haven't lured them into my den by telling them about lobbing chuckies in the loch when I was a wee lad.

Lorna (*offstage*) Phil!

Phil In the kitchen!

Kev You know that's not what I meant.

Lorna (*offstage*) I'm going shopping! Want to come?

Phil More than anything! Lorna loves me. She may not remember my birthday, but she loves me. And I love her.

Kev I wasn't making a judgement. I was just saying that our experiences are very different. Have become very different.

Lorna *enters. She looks even more stylish than earlier.* **Phil** *smiles admiringly.*

Phil Look at you. Shop assistants will produce things from the stockroom they didn't even know they had.

She beams at **Kev**.

Lorna Phil is the only man on earth who likes watching a woman buy clothes.

Phil I don't *mind* it.

Lorna You get a hard-on!

Phil (*with pride*) Lorna Gaffney. A world without secrets. (*Turning to* **Kev**, *far from thawed.*) I want to see Betty and Jess, so we'll nip back later. Just for a bit. Then we'll head off again for dinner.

Kev OK.

Lorna   Have you had a row?

Phil   We're mid-flow.

Lorna   Do you want to finish it?

Phil   I'm not in the mood. Are you?

Kev   No.

Kev salutes a goodbye to her. **Phil** *nods goodbye to* **Kev**. **Phil** *and* **Lorna** *exit. Sound of front door opening and shutting.* **Kev** *looks burdened. He starts to clear up. He stops. He takes out his phone, gets a number up and calls it all in one action – he knows a pause will undo the impulse.*

Kev   Fay. It's Kev again. I know you're doing the presentation and I don't want to hound you, just . . . call me, would you? Whenever you can. Call me. Ta.

He ends the call. He knows his voice betrayed nerves and need. He chucks his phone onto a cluttered surface. He begins to clear up the kitchen, with angry speed.

Blackout.

Scene Three

Lights up. The kitchen is clean and tidy. The light through the window is fading. **Jane** *and* **Kev** *sit side by side on the sofa. At their feet, with sleek wet hair, sit* **Jess** *and* **Betty**. **Kev** *and* **Jane** *each hold a small, fine-toothed comb and are going through each child's head of hair in search of nits. After each go-through, they check their comb to see if they've extracted a nit. They then wipe the comb on kitchen paper and start the process again. For each nit found in their hair,* **Betty** *and* **Jess** *are awarded a Smartie.*

Jane   Ooh. That's a whopper.

Betty *watches miserably as* **Jane** *plinks a Smartie into* **Jess**'s *saucer, already containing about ten.* **Betty**'s *is empty.*

Betty   You are *so* lucky!

Jane   Well, I think you're pretty lucky not to have nits.

Jess   Mrs Friar says nits is wrong. It's the eggs that are nits.

Jane   It's the empty eggs that are the nits, she's right. And what we call nits should really be called headlice. But what would you rather have crawling about on your head? Lice or nits?

Jess   Nits!

Jane   Exactly.

Betty   I don't care what they're called as long as I've got some.

Jane *plinks two more Smarties into* **Jess***'s saucer.* **Betty** *starts to cry.*

Kev   Ah, Betty, come on. Let's go and rinse you off, you're clean as a whistle.

Jane   Have you tried right underneath at the back?

Kev   I've tried everywhere.

Jane   I do this twice a week and that's where I usually find them.

Kev *looks at her, annoyed, then combs through underneath the back of* **Betty***'s hair.*

Kev   Nothing.

Jane   I think that's you done, Jess.

Jess   Let me count them all up. I'm very glad I saved them till the end.

She starts to count out her Smarties. **Betty** *glowers.* **Kev** *continues with his annoyed combing.*

Jess   One, two, three, four, five, six, seven, eight, nine, ten –

Kev   Jesus Christ.

*He is studying his comb, fresh from its last trawl. He pours a stream of Smarties into **Betty**'s saucer.*

Betty   Yes! Yes! Yes! Yes! Yes!

*Everyone laughs. **Betty** delightedly fills her mouth with them.*

Jess   Stop! You don't know how many you've got! How many did she get?

Betty   (*mouth full*)   Lots.

Kev   (*still studying comb, awed*)   This one is massive. This is the daddy.

*He shows it to **Betty** and **Jess**, who are impressed. **Jess** posts a Smartie into **Kev**'s mouth, then one into **Jane**'s mouth.*

Jane   Thank you, my darling.

Betty *and* **Jess** *clamber up onto the sofa and sprawl over their parents.* **Betty** *snuggles up, with one hand cupping one of* **Jane**'s *breasts and the thumb of her other hand clamped in her mouth.* **Jess** *and* **Kev** *are exchanging kisses on the lips, taking it in turns to initiate.* **Betty** *has a good squeeze of* **Jane**'s *breast.*

Betty   You're nice and squashy.

Jane   Thanks, darling.

Jess   Mum. Kiss.

Jane *and* **Jess** *exchange kisses on the lips.* **Kev** *strokes* **Jess**'s *back.* **Betty** *fondles* **Jane**'s *breast.* **Jane** *accepts a kiss from* **Kev**, *somewhat tentatively.*

Jess   This is family.

They all remain heaped together, each holding on to some part of all three others.

I'm never going to leave home.

Jane   You will.

Jess   I won't.

Kev   You will.

Jess If I do, I'll live next door. And I will come home for every meal and you will cook me eggy-bread.

Betty (*at length*) Dad?

Kev Yeah.

Betty This day, in the morning, when we were getting ready for school, Mum hit Jess.

Kev (*looking at* **Jane**, *amazed*) Did she?

Betty Yeah. Actually she didn't just hit her, she actually really whacked her.

Kev Is that true?

Jane Yes.

Jess Betty! We're not supposed to tell!

Kev You hit her?

Betty Made a big red mark.

Kev Jesus. Why didn't you tell me?

Jane Because I was ashamed. I apologised as soon as I picked her up from school.

Jess I was only telling her not to be nasty to Betty and she whacked me.

Jane They were driving me crazy.

Kev How hard did you hit her?

Jess Very hard.

Kev Shhh. Hmm?

Jane Hard.

Kev Hard as you hit me?

Jane Yes.

Kev Bloody hell, Jane!

Betty When did you hit Dad?

Jane   This morning.

Betty   Why?

Jess   Why did you hit Dad, Mum?

Jane   Because he said something.

Jess   What did you say?

Kev   You'll have to ask Mum.

Jane   I can't remember.

Uproar.

Betty *and* **Jess**   Rubbish! / That's not true! / Tell us! / That's a lie! (*Etc.*)

Jane   Ssssh. Sh-sh-sh-sh. It doesn't matter. It was a grown-up thing.

Jess   *I want to know.*

Kev   I wonder if . . . anybody wants . . . a present.

Betty *and* **Jess**   Me! / Me! / Me!

Kev   Well. If you go upstairs into me and Mum's bedroom, and you look in the side pocket of my big bag, you will find two presents.

Betty   Are they both the same?

Kev   Exactly the same.

Betty *and* **Jess** *thunder out.*

Jess (*offstage*)   Thanks, Dad.

Kev *turns to* **Jane***, wide-eyed.*

Kev   What's going on here?

Jane   It's been happening for a couple of months. I never mean to. I'm sorry.

Kev   Why are you hitting them?

Jane   I'm not happy.

He stares at her, amazed.

Kev How long haven't you been happy?

Jane Months.

Kev When did you stop telling me things?

Jane I think it's what I do to stop myself needing you.

Kev I want you to need me!

Jane There is point needing you when you're not here. So I stop myself needing you by holding things back.

Kev That just shuts me out.

Jane Going away so much shuts me out.

Kev I've got to work. I've got to earn. I hate going away so much. I'd love to be at home more.

Jane I'd love to go on trains and stay in hotels and have colleagues. And fall in love with them. I'd love to be you. You do what you've always done.

Kev (*very stung*) We made a deal. We discussed it endlessly. I would carry on working because I liked my job and you would knock yours on the head because you didn't –

Jane When we made the deal I didn't know what it would do to me!

Kev So get a job! Betty's started school – now's the time. God knows we could do with the money.

Jane I've looked at jobs. It's hopeless.

Kev What do you want to do?

Jane I don't know. I don't know anything. I don't know the difference between Congress and the Senate. I don't know if the sun goes round the moon or the earth. I used to know. I can't keep asking. What's the point of being here if I don't know how it works? I know the world is foul. I know it's full of bombs and shanty towns, but I'm stuck in my box because I don't know enough to clamber out. Why haven't I read a book for five years? I don't know.

She is crying. Amazed, **Kev** *goes to her.*

Kev   Jane. Jane. Don't be sad. Please.

He holds her, her head bent into him.

When I'm away, I often wish I was you. Wish I could be here when the girls want to show me something or tell me something. Wish I could be in our bed. Have tea in my mug.

She wriggles clear of him.

Jane   Your life is better.

Kev   I love being at home.

Jane   It's hell. You've got no idea. You think it's safe. It's not.

Kev   We'll sort all this out. You might not know now what you want to do but you will, and when you do, you must do it. Re-train, go back to college – whatever it takes. But don't be unhappy.

Jane   I will sort it out! Don't be nice to me! I'm really pissed off with you. (*She glares at him.*) I should have told you how it was. I won't do it any more. I decided on my walk. From now on I'm going to tell you things.

Kev   Good.

Jane   If we don't need each other, we're sunk.

Kev   I agree.

Jane   I'm going to tell you everything.

Kev   What sort of things? Bad things?

Jane   True things.

Jess *hurtles in.*

Jess   Mum! Dad gave us torches!

Jane Lucky you!

Jess *stands against* **Kev***, holding his leg.*

Jess Thanks, Dad. When will it be dark?

Kev Soon.

Jane After tea it'll be dark.

Jess Mum. Betty wants you. She's broken her torch.

Jane Has she got the batteries out?

Jess Yes. And a springy thing.

Jane (*exiting*) Jesus.

Jess *blows her cheeks out.* **Kev** *pushes them flat to produce a fart sound. They do this three times.*

Jess I'm glad you're home.

Kev Me too.

Jess Dad.

Kev Yes.

Jess I know how you make a baby.

Kev Do you?

Jess Yes. I do. You have to sex.

Kev That's right.

Jess What is it?

Kev It's a special kind of hug.

Jess Show me.

Kev I can't.

Jess Why?

Kev You're the wrong size.

Jess When will I be the right size?

Kev When you're about twenty.

Jess   That's long away.

Kev   Yes. But you will never be the right size for me.

Jess   Why?

Kev   'Cause I'm your dad.

Jess *nods, still unclear.*

Jess   Will I have a hairy fanny?

Kev   Yes.

Betty *hurtles in, holding her torch.*

Betty   It's absolutely fine. I didn't break it.

Jess   Is that yours?

Betty   Yes!

Jess   Where's mine?

Betty   In your bedroom!

Jess   I don't believe you, Betty!

Jess, *scowling with suspicion, runs off.*

Betty   Dad.

Kev   Yes.

Betty   Dad.

Kev   Yes.

Betty   The thing is, Dad, I don't want to die.

Kev   Don't worry about that, sweetheart.

Betty   But I don't want to! I don't want you to die, either.

Kev   People live for ages nowadays, Betty. In the olden days people died much younger. You can live till you're a hundred now.

Betty   Will you?

Kev   I hope so. I expect so. Yes, I will.

Her anguish shows no sign of abating.

Betty   But what happens after? Why don't they know? Mrs Bristol says you go to Heaven and God gives you a nice cup of tea.

Kev   I like the sound of that.

Betty   I don't like tea!

Kev   Ask for juice.

Betty   Yes. I'll ask for apple juice. Paige in Year One says sometimes they put you in a box in the ground, and sometimes they put you in a box and burn you! But what if you've been good?

He sees how frantic she is becoming. It makes him feel frantic too.

Kev   Betty, don't listen to Paige in Year One. Don't think about these things. Don't worry about it, it's a million miles away.

Betty   I told Yasmin in Year Two Hell was rubbish, but she said it isn't. She said Hell is hotter than invinity. But why do you get burned again when you were already burneded in the box?

Kev   You don't! Betty, you don't! None of this is true.

Betty   I bloody don't want to die!

She flings her arms around him, weeping. He sits, with her crying form heaped on him. He looks about at his kitchen, shaken and out of his depth. **Jane** *enters.*

Jane   (*quiet*)   What's up?

Kev   Mortality.

Jane *nods and starts to fix tea. She sets about chopping up carrot sticks, toasting pitta bread, dolloping houmous onto plates.* **Kev** *watches her.*

Kev   These things you're going to tell me.

Jane   Yes.

Kev   When's that going to happen?

Jane   Tonight. We'll get them to bed early.

She takes the lid off the bin, to chuck away carrot waste. It's full. She heaves out the full bag, ties it up and exits. **Kev** *bends his head to* **Betty***.*

Kev   Are you feeling any better?

Betty   I don't want to go to bed early.

Jess *darts in.*

Jess   I'm starving! Starving, starving, starving!

Kev   Tea's ready. Come and sit.

He lays **Betty** *down on the sofa, and quickly sets the table.* **Betty** *watches, sucking her thumb.* **Jess** *filches carrot sticks and pokes the houmous while* **Kev***'s back is turned.*

Kev   Oy! Wait! Come and sit down, don't snatch it off the plates.

Jess   I need to eat! Now!

Jane *re-enters. Tea is clattered onto the table.* **Jess** *eats hungrily.*

Jane   Come on, Betty.

Betty   I'm not hungry.

Kev   Try it and see. You might feel like it if you try some.

The doorbell rings. **Jess** *jumps up, food forgotten.*

Jess   Phil!

Jane   Shh. Sit down. Dad'll go.

Kev *goes to open the front door.* **Betty** *and* **Jess** *stand and look after him – hounds alert to the imminent appearance of outsiders.*

Jane   Come on, sit down.

Betty   I'm going to be shy.

Jane   That's a shame. (*To* **Jess***.*) What are you going to be?

Jess   Normal.

Jane   Jolly good.

Phil and **Lorna** enter. **Lorna** carries a small bag from a very expensive shop. **Phil** carries a plain, bright plastic bag. **Kev** follows behind. In response to his own annoyance with **Kev**, the frostiness directed from **Jane** to **Lorna** and the unease between **Kev** and **Jane**, **Phil** becomes increasingly cranked up as this scene progresses.

Phil   Hello, ladies.

Lorna   Uhhh! They're huge! Didn't you get big? Hello, I'm Lorna, you probably don't remember.

Silence.

Jane   What do you say, girls?

Betty flattens her body against **Jane**'s and buries her face. **Phil** slings his jacket over the back of a chair.

Jess   Hello.

Jane (to **Phil**)   Betty's going to be shy. She just warned us.

Betty (shouting into **Jane**'s clothing)   DON'T SAY THAT!

Phil   It's very smart, Betty. Always have a social strategy.

Jane peels **Betty** off and sits her at the table.

Jane   Come on, girls, eat.

Kev (to **Lorna** only)   How was shopping?

Lorna   Good.

Phil (to **Jane** only)   She shopped till I dropped.

Lorna (to **Kev** only)   I bought a dress.

Jess and **Betty** look, as one, with undivided interest at **Lorna**.

Lorna   Oh that got your attention! Shall I show it to you?

Jess (jumping up)   Yes!

Jane   No, no, no. After tea. They need to have their tea.

Lorna makes a face to **Kev** that momentarily communicates both 'I've just been told off,' and 'Your wife's uptight.'

Jane   Well, I'm sorry, but they do. And if there's a lot of excitement it's hopeless.

Lorna   I just bring excitement wherever I go. I can't help it.

Kev *admires the cheek.* **Jane** *is boot-faced.*

Phil (*of food*)   Ooh! Look at this! You lucky girls.

He helps himself to some, as do all the adults.

So how was school?

Jess   Fine.

Phil   Betty?

Betty *shoots him a dirty look.*

Phil   Did you learn anything?

Jess   Yes. Mrs Bristol told us something interesting. She said –

Betty (*loud and clear*)   I had a very hard day.

Jess   Hey! I was talking! –

Betty   He asked me! –

Jane   Oy! Stop it!

Phil   Let's start with Mrs Bristol.

Jess   Don't want to now.

Phil *looks at* **Jane***: 'Sorry.'* **Lorna** *heads into the yard for a cigarette.*

Phil   Tell me about your hard day, then, Betty.

Kev   Come on, Betty. What did you do?

Betty   Literacy.

Kev   What else?

Betty   Numeracy.

Kev   What else?

Betty   Lunch.

Phil   What did you have?

Betty   Nuffink.

Phil   Who did you sit next to?

Betty   Nobody.

Phil   Excellent. Jess, I'm dying to know what Mrs Bristol said, please tell me.

Jess (*at length*)   She said you've got to be nice to ugly-faced people.

Phil   I totally agree.

Jess   It's what's inside that counts.

Phil   Mrs Bristol's absolutely right. I always do that. Well, look, I'm being nice to you, aren't I?

Jess (*smiling*)   I'm not ugly. (*She beams through the following.*)

Phil   You? With your big blue eyes and your little white teeth and your soft pink cheeks – you're hideous!

Jess's *face falls. She shoves her chair back and storms out of the room.*

Phil   Jess! Jess! It was a joke!

He goes after her.

Jess (*offstage*)   GO AWAY!

Lorna (*appearing in doorway from yard*)   He's a natural.

Jane *exits.*

Jane (*offstage*)   Come on, Jess, it was funny!

Phil *re-enters, head in hands.*

Phil   What an arse.

Kev *waves it away.* **Lorna**'s *disappeared back out into the yard.*

Kev (*making sure* **Betty**'s *preoccupied with eating, unable to keep his anxiety to himself*)   Jane says she's going to tell me things.

Phil   Right.

Jess (*offstage*)   PHIL IS A HORRIBLE MAN!

Kev   What d'you think she's going to tell me?

Phil   I don't know.

Kev   I've got to wait till –

He does a mime of sleep, nods at **Betty**.

Kev   It's unbearable.

Phil *dips into his jacket pocket for his inhaler.* **Lorna** *reappears from the yard and bins her cigarette end.*

Betty   What have you got for us?

Kev   Betty. That's very rude.

Betty   I bet they've got us something.

Phil   We have.

Betty   What is it?

Phil   My assistant will show you.

Lorna   Will I get strips torn off me if I do?

Kev *shakes his head that she won't.* **Phil** *has a puff on his inhaler and returns it to pocket of jacket slung over chair. Meanwhile,* **Lorna** *takes from the bright plastic bag two feather boas, one pink, one purple.* **Betty** *is enraptured.*

Betty   Jess! Come and see! We've got more presents!

Jess *enters, blotchy-faced, followed by* **Jane**. **Jess** *gasps at the beauty of the boas, which* **Lorna** *is modelling with some panache.*

Kev   What do you say, girls?

Betty   Who gets the pink one?

Jane   THAT IS NOT WHAT YOU SAY!

Everyone is shocked.

Betty *and* **Jess**   Thank you.

Lorna   You're welcome. Jess, d'you want to see my new dress?

Jess *nods.* **Lorna** *goes to her expensive shop bag and shakes out, from tissue paper, a dress. It is sheer and floaty. If you scrunched it up it would fit in your pocket. It has a soft pattern, predominantly purple.*

Jess   I want the purple one.

Jane   When you've finished eating.

Jess   Put it on.

Lorna   I will. Phil's taking me out for cocktails tonight.

Betty   What's cocktails?

Phil   A cocktail is a fruity drink that makes you talk a lot and then fall over.

Lorna   I'll go and put it on.

She exits, leaving both boas behind. **Jane**, *rattled, picks at leftovers.*

Jane   If I had my time again I'd be high-maintenance.

Phil   Would you?

Jane   Yeah.

Phil   Wouldn't suit you.

Jane   If I'd started early enough it would. I'd have become it. Had my first facial at fourteen and never looked back. And I'd have behaved much worse because you're allowed to if you're high maintenance. Stand people up. Let people pay for you. Dick people around. Never send a Christmas card to an ex-boyfriend's mother . . .

Kev   I don't think I'd have liked you.

Jane   I don't suppose you'd have been in the frame.

Kev   What are you trying to say?

Phil   I think it's a wee dig at Lorna.

Kev   It's a dig at me.

Jane   It's just a bit of whimsy.

Kev   With teeth.

Kev *and* **Jane** *hold a hostile look.*

Phil   Soon as Lorna's ready, we'll head out. This is just a pit-stop. Just wanted to see the girls. And scar Jess for life.

Betty   Dad, can I watch telly?

Kev   Well, not for long. Got to get you in the bath.

Betty   Come on.

Kev (*wiping her face*)   Hang on. Finished, Jess?

Jess   No. (*She continues eating.*)

Betty (*arms up*)   Carry!

Kev *carries* **Betty** *out.* **Betty** *scoops up the pink boa as she goes.*

Phil   How are you doing?

Jane (*indicating* **Jess**)   Hard to say at present.

Phil   I always forget. That's quality surveillance though, isn't it? To be so unobtrusive. Most spies make the mistake of being fully grown.

Jess *looks at him, suspecting she is the subject of this gibberish.*

Phil   Jess. I'm sorry I'm a horrible man. Tell me something. Do you have a boyfriend?

Jess (*delighted outrage*)   No!

Phil   You must do. A lovely girl like you.

Jess   Well, I do like Tony Bokhari.

Phil   Oh yes?

Jess   He's brown. He's got a nice smile. Me and Kimberley saw him in the playground and we thought he looked nice so we went up to him and called him names.

Phil   That was Lorna's approach! What did you call him?

Jess (*progressively self-amused*)   Tony Bucket-head. Tony T-shirt. Tony Chair. Tony Girl.

Phil   Excellent.

Jess   I want to watch telly now.

Jane   Just a sec.

Jane *wipes* **Jess***'s face.* **Jess** *runs off, scooping up the purple boa as she goes.*

Jane (*urgent*)   I'm going to tell Kev.

Phil   About – ?

He flicks his finger towards her and then back to him. She nods.

Jane   You're right. It is the right thing to do.

Phil   I didn't say that.

Jane   You implied it. Anyway it is. And I'm going to.

Phil   Well. Good luck.

Silence as both are lost in their own trains of nervous thought.

Did Lorna piss you off this morning? She said she thought she did.

Jane   I don't think Lorna's a good idea.

Phil   In what way?

Jane   I don't think she's nice enough.

Phil   God, who is!

Jane   For you. I don't think she's nice enough for you. I think she's toying with you.

Phil   What man alive wouldn't want to be toyed with by Lorna?

Jane   The best ones wouldn't. You shouldn't.

Phil   Oh Jane. This is confusing. I feel flattered and told off at the same time. Which feeling should I go with?

Jane   I can see she's intoxicating, but I don't think she's . . . I don't think she's a worthy custodian of your heart.

He laughs at her earnestness.

Phil   Me-and-Lorna has its own logic, and in its own perverse way it's wholesome. Lorna unnerves people because she doesn't care what they think. She beats her own path. That's what I love about her.

Jane   She's brutal.

Phil   That's bracing! (*He looks at* **Jane** *for a moment.*) I know there are kinder women, women gentler on the nervous system . . . But they don't seem to be what the gods have in mind for me.

Jane *looks at him, about to speak.*

Kev (*offstage*)   Jane!

Jane   Yeah?

Kev (*offstage*)   I want these kids in the bath in ten minutes, OK?

Jane   OK!

Betty (*offstage*)   Mum! Mum! (*She shoots in.*) There's something scary on the telly. I'm frightened.

Jane   Dad's there.

Betty   I need you.

Phil   And me.

Betty   No. Not you.

Jane   Come on.

Jane *takes* **Betty**'s *hand. All three exit. Long moment.* **Jess** *enters. She hops up on the table and enjoys a little agitation in private.* **Lorna** *enters. She is wearing her new dress. She carries a jacket.*

Jess (*without breaking her rhythm*)   You look beautiful.

Lorna   I did it for you.

Jess   That jacket won't look beautiful.

Lorna   This is Phil's. So he can look as beautiful as me.

Jess *nods, growing pinker with exertion.*

Lorna   What are you doing?

Jess   This.

Lorna   What is it?

Jess   It's what I do.

Lorna   Does it feel nice?

Jess   Yes.

Lorna   Good on you. Well, we're off now, Jess. See you tomorrow.

Jess *nods.* **Lorna** *starts to go.*

Jess   What's your name?

Lorna   Lorna.

Jess   Lorna, do you have a hairy fanny?

Lorna   No darlin', I shave.

Jess   Cool.

Lorna *sweeps out.* **Jess** *continues.*

Kev (*offstage*)   Jess! Bath time! Now!

Jess *runs out.*

Blackout.

Scene Four

Lights up. Outside the kitchen window is a dark winter night. **Jane** *enters and goes to the sink to fill two plastic beakers with water.* **Kev** *enters, at a lick, angry.*

Kev   Why are you doing this?

Jane   Because I think we should.

Kev   But why did you agree to it?

Jane   Because they want to. It won't take long.

Kev   This is punishment. You're making me hang on as long as possible before you tell me whatever it is you're going to tell me!

Jane   If we stuff them in bed now, they'll bounce back out in ten minutes. Calm down.

Kev   I'm agitated for good reason!

Betty *enters, in her pyjamas. She carries her torch. She drags a chair and stands on it to turn one set of lights off.* **Jess** *enters – also in pyjamas, also carrying her torch. Both have damp, washed hair. Both are brimming with excitement.*

Kev   This has got to be quick, OK?

Betty *and* **Jess**   OK!

Jess   Please take your seats, sirs and madams. The show is about to begin.

Jane *and* **Kev** *settle on the sofa.*

Kev   Quick, yeah?

Jess   Yes!

Betty   Ready?

Betty *switches off the second set of lights. The kitchen is plunged into darkness.*

Jess   Welcome to the Spooky Dark Show!

Jane   Wooo, this is very spooky already.

Betty   I can't find my switch!

Jess (*whispered*)   Here.

One torch lights up.

Not now!

Betty   Sorry!

Torch goes out.

Jess   Welcome to the Spooky Dark Show!

Kev (*under breath*)   Yes yes yes.

One torch comes on.

Jane   Woooo.

The other torch comes on.

Kev   Woooo.

The moves of the show are as follows: **Jess** *and* **Betty** *shine torches in each other's faces while making terrifying expressions. Torches are put inside mouths and orange light shines through cheeks. Torches are shone behind ears and orange light shines through them. Torches are shone rapidly round the kitchen, momentarily lighting up* **Kev** *and* **Jane**'s *faces. Her expression is dutifully terror-struck, his is impatient. The finale is a bare bum, probably* **Betty**'s, *brightly torchlit for a second.*

Hearty applause. **Kev** *flicks on the lights.*

Kev   Fantastic!

Jess   There's more!

Kev   No, that was just right.

Jess   I want to do more!

Betty *makes a break for the light switch.*

Kev   No!

Betty *switches the light off.*

Kev   Put it back on!

Betty   No!

Kev   Put it back on! Betty.

The lights come back on.

Betty   You've ruined everything!

Kev   It was a great show and now it's time for bed.

Great moans from **Betty** *and* **Jess**.

Jess (*sternly examining the torch in her hand*)   Betty, this is not my torch.

Betty   It is.

Jess   You've chewed it.

Betty   That's your torch.

Jess   It is not.

Betty   It's in your hand so who does that make its?

Jess *runs at* **Betty**, *who curls up to resist torch-snatching.*

Jane   Stop it!

Kev   Hey hey hey!

Jess *whacks* **Betty**.

Kev   STOP IT!

He has everyone's attention.

There is to be *no more hitting* in this house *ever − by anyone*. Is that understood?

He surveys his womenfolk. They nod.

Jess   You frightened me with that shouting.

Kev   Say sorry for hitting Betty.

Jess   Sorry.

Kev   Not to me.

Jess *turns to* **Betty**.

Jess   Sorry.

Kev   Give Jess her tor −

Betty   It's not −

Kev   *Give her her torch.* (*He swaps the torches.*) OK. No gloating. No whining. Bed.

Jess *gives* **Jane** *a tragic kiss.* **Betty** *drops to all fours and pads towards the door.* **Kev** *collects the beakers of water.*

Jane Kiss?

Betty *shakes her head.* **Jess** *and* **Kev** *exit, followed by* **Betty**. **Jane** *goes to* **Phil**'s *box of wine, takes a bottle, opens it and pours two glasses. She takes a single cigarette from a hiding place. She opens the door to the yard and stands half-outside, edgily puffing and sipping.* **Kev** *enters, takes his wine.*

Kev I feel like I've been waiting to be hanged. Tell me.

Jane I will sort out what I want to do and who I'm going to be.

Kev Good.

They drink.

Jane Also, don't tell Fay how you feel about her – 'cause if you pursue her like you pursued me, you'll get her. So please don't.

Kev *scowls into his drink.*

Jane I think if you really wanted to work away less, you could.

Kev Point taken. I'll look into it.

They drink.

Jane And the other thing is: I know what it's like to have feelings for someone else. It happened to me.

Kev I don't want to know.

Jane Well, I want to tell. Six years ago when I was pregnant with Jess –

Kev I told her! I told her last night! I told Fay I'm in love with her! I said, 'I'm in love with you!'

Kev *is a helpless conduit. Words leap from his mouth like people from a burning building.*

Jane What did she say?

Kev She said, 'I know.' She said, 'I know, but don't worry because I'm in love with you, too.'

Jane (*catching the rising hysteria*)   What happened then?

Kev   I got in the car and drove home! I panicked! I don't know what I was doing! What was I thinking? It's you I want! I lost my wits! I want you!

Jane   Well, maybe I don't want you! Why don't you get in the car and drive back? See if you can face up to sex with her. Go to Fay. It'd be weeks before Jess and Betty even noticed! (*Angry tears coming.*) You told me you hadn't told her!

Kev   Forgive me.

Jane   Stupid man. Fucking stupid man.

Kev *holds his head, miserable. She drinks. She thinks.*

Jane (*in a conscientiously level tone – 'before I was so rudely interrupted'*)   Six years ago when I was pregnant with Jess, Phil came round. And when he stood next to me – exactly where you're standing now – I got the shakes.

Kev *emits a miniscule moan.*

Jane   It'd never happened before, but I felt a lot of funny things when I was pregnant – I could smell the kitchen bin from the front door, d'you remember?

Kev   Yes, but it's not on a par.

Jane   Anyway, I put it down to being pregnant. So. I had Jess. But nothing changed. I waited for it to go away but it didn't. It went on for two years.

More body-buckling from **Kev**.

Jane   One night when you were away in Cardiff, Phil was over for dinner and I blurted it out.

Kev *hunches further into himself.*

Jane   He told me to go to bed. He said he'd have taken it as a compliment if I hadn't been so drunk. Which I was. I think I must have done it on purpose because it was an awful secret to carry around.

Kev   Why didn't you tell *me*?

Jane I didn't think you'd understand. So he went home. And I went to bed. And I cried. I made screechy in-and-out noises like a donkey. I felt – *so* – *stupid* and *lonely*. And bad. Next morning, I woke up, sick as a dog but better. Not cured. But nothing trembly or hopeful left. Just a very very shitty feeling. Which I felt I deserved so it was almost gratifying. And gradually, by plunging back down as deeply as I could into all the ordinary things I'd had a holiday from –

Kev – like me.

Jane Yes. And Jess. And having Betty. And it eased. Phil didn't come here for a year. You visited him but he didn't come here till your birthday party. And it was all right.

Kev *uncurls himself from his ball and stares at her.*

Kev Jesus Christ, Jane, you're full of surprises.

She drinks.

You seem to want to hurt me.

Jane I do.

Kev You're supposed to be the nice one.

Jane I don't want to be.

Kev What if I hadn't told you about Fay? Would you have kept quiet?

Jane I don't know.

Kev We said we'd tell.

Noiselessly barefoot, **Jess** *has entered.* **Jane** *hurls her cigarette into the yard.*

Jess Were you smoking a cigarette?

Jane Err . . .

Jess Your lung will go black and they'll put it in a bucket.

Jane What's up?

Jess   You didn't put us to bed in a nice way.

Jane   Sorry about that. Night-night.

Jess *exits reluctantly. They wait for her to travel out of earshot.*

Kev   Seems the only thing that stopped you was being knocked back. What if he'd been into you?

Jane   He'd never be into me. He likes Anglepoise lamps like Lorna.

Kev   But if he *had* been into you. You'd have fucked him. You wanted to.

Jane   I wanted to drive in his van and walk round Loch Lomond with him –

Kev   – Come on!

Jane   – and have sex with him. I had sex with him in dreams all over the place. Staircases, trains, fields, our bed. And every time – both of us straining towards ecstasy, this – *thing* – like a headline made of lead would smash down on top of us: KEV. My *subconscious* was monogamous; I couldn't even fuck him in my sleep.

Kev (*furious*)   You can't know what you would have done.

Jess *reappears.*

Jess   Mum. You forgot to take my letter to Mrs Friar into school.

Jane   We'll take it in on Monday.

Jess   Where is it?

Jane   It's there. It's safe. We'll take it in on Monday.

Jess   I want to hear what you're saying.

Jane   Go to bed!

Jess *pouts off. Pause.*

Kev   We were fine at the time, weren't we?

Jane   I think so.

Kev You gave nothing away.

Jane Nothing you noticed.

Kev What does that *say*? All that going on for two years and I never knew!

Jess *stands in the doorway.*

Kev Jesus wept. What?

Jess What didn't you know was going on?

Kev Doesn't matter. This is Mum and Dad time. Go to bed.

Jess Tell me what you're saying. It sounds important.

Kev Jess. Go to bed. Don't want to see you till morning.

Jess THIS IS MY HOUSE! YOU JUST LIVE IN IT!

She stomps off.

Kev Phil can talk about anything. He can talk about buddleia. He always has something funny to say, or neat. But if you try and go anywhere deeper – if you try and access the messy stuff, you just get more – neat talk. He's zero.

Jane (*shocked*) He's your best friend.

Kev Why's he still living like a student, aged forty-one? Why's he content to be a glorified removal man? He's got a bit missing that's made him – get stuck.

Jane I didn't fall for him because he's better than you.

Kev Does he still give you the shakes?

Betty (*offstage*) Mum!

Jane Go to bed, Jess!

Betty *appears.*

Kev Betty! God help me! What is it?

Betty I had a bad dream! This monster creeped into my room and it bited me and I runned but I falled and it catched me and putted me in a sack and then I shrinked and then I woke up!

Jane   I don't think you've even been asleep yet.

Kev   Go to bed.

Betty   You look duspicious.

Jane   Do I?

Betty   What does duspicious mean?

Jane   Go to bed.

Betty *makes to go, turns back.*

Betty   When you die, do you wake up?

Jane   Yes.

Betty   My cover's come off.

Jane   Bloody hell. Come on.

Jane *leads* **Betty** *out.* **Kev** *looks about wildly, less and less able to make sense of his world. He drinks.*

A key sounds in the front door, footsteps approach. **Phil** *enters, jauntily drunk.*

Phil   Never change your jacket without checking your pockets.

He rifles in the jacket slung over the back of a chair and removes his inhaler.

I've had a bad day for breathing.

He has a puff on his inhaler.

Jane still putting them to bed?

Kev *manages a nod.*

Phil   God, those cocktails are strong. Feel like I've got feathers for feet. Jumped a cab and London looked like Koyanisqatsi. Try saying that when you're sober. We just bumped into an old friend of Lorna's from art school. Lives in Amsterdam. Very nice guy. I'd love to live in Amsterdam.

Kev *is a thing of jealousy. Breathing, speaking and standing are all proving difficult.*

Phil Well. I'd best get back to them. See you in the morning.

He makes to go.

Kev Jane tells me that for two years you were her number-one pin-up.

Phil Oh God. Is that – all right?

Kev It's still sinking in.

Phil What was she thinking? I don't mean telling, I mean pinning me up?

Kev That's what I wondered. I want to kill you twice. Once for giving my wife the shakes. Once for thinking she wasn't good enough.

Phil (*laughing*) Well, thereby hangs a tale.

Long pause. **Kev** *looks at* **Phil**, *transfixed.*

Phil Am I going to tell you this? No. Yes, fuck it I am. And it's funny. It actually is quite funny. When Jane told me what she told me all those years ago, sitting at this very table, I was astonished. I'd never fancied her. I love her, but, as you know, I prefer a leggier lady. So it was a strange thing, but mainly a drunken thing. So anyway, I went home and I went to bed and I lay there and I thought how reckless it had been to tell me. How unlike her. How daring and brave and impulsive and – *hot*. This is the incredible thing. Before she told me, she was a nice woman who had your babies. After she told me she became this – *siren*. For weeks she just sizzled in my head. I had the *corniest* fantasies about her. You know –

Kev I don't want to know!

Phil It was bizarre. And I kept thinking, 'Is this all it takes? A show of interest from a woman with acceptable hip width?' I was really worried. I could see the mess brewing.

And then I thought, 'Just take control. It's all about control' –
I really believe that. So I avoided her. Didn't go near her
for nearly a year. And it passed.

Kev *is flabbergasted.*

Phil   You are never, ever, to tell Jane that, OK? I'm
serious. D'you swear?

Kev *nods.*

Kev   And – wh – what's it like now?

Phil   I'm fine unless she wears her purple cords.

Kev   What happens then?

Phil   I have inappropriate thoughts.

Kev   Oh God.

Phil   But probably no more than you have about Lorna.
It's not an accident I don't have a bank account, you know.
Painting murals and driving a van isn't a fuck-up. It's my
little system. I could have worn a suit but I chose not to.
I could have had your wife but I chose not to.

Kev *shoves* **Phil** *extremely hard.* **Phil** *shoves him back, equally
forcefully.*

Phil   You fall for a woman at work and the whole world
comes to a standstill! Everyone has to know! You think
you're a man of the world. You're a Buildings Safety
Inspector! You travel to Plymouth! Portsmouth! Cardiff! You
wheel your Samsonite into shitty little hotels all over nowhere
feeling like a big shot!

Kev *shoves* **Phil** *again.*

Phil   Don't shove me like a little prick. Hit me. Do you
want to hit me? Hit me. I'd love to hit you back.

Kev *wants to hit* **Phil** *but won't give* **Phil** *the satisfaction. His
arms, charged up, shoot above his head and judder as if a strong
electric current is passing through them.* **Phil** *watches, amazed.* **Kev**
regains control of his arms and, panting, takes a long drink. **Phil** *puffs
on his inhaler.*

Jane *enters, wearing purple cords.*

Jane (*surprised*)   Hello.

Phil (*holding up his inhaler*)   I came back for this.

Kev   You've changed your clothes.

Jane   She spilt her water all over me.

The two men stare at her.

What?

Phil   Nothing. I just came back for this.

Kev   Jane is wearing her purple cords, Phil.

Phil   I see that.

Kev   How's it going?

Jane *looks from* **Kev** *to* **Phil**, *lost.*

Kev   Phil fancies the arse off you in those.

Jane *looks amazed.*

Kev   It's true. He just told me.

Phil   That's not what I said. I do think you look great in them as it goes.

Kev   He said he had inappropriate thoughts when you wear them.

Jane   I don't understand what's going on.

Kev   He didn't used to fancy you, but once you'd told him you'd fallen for him, he got the hots for you.

Phil   Jane. Sorry. Kev. You are an evil bastard. You just promised me you wouldn't tell her that.

Kev   Jane. Sorry. I hope this isn't embarrassing for you.

Jane   No, it's cheering me up. It's good for morale.

Kev   He's my best friend.

Jane   Is he? He just called you a zero.

Phil   A zero?

Jane *nods.* **Phil** *looks at* **Kev***, deeply wounded.*

Jane   At least Phil knew how to keep his mouth shut at the time, Kev. Had some discretion. Turns out he did tell Fay he's in love with her. Last night. Then he jumped in the car and came home to take a day to get round to admitting as much.

Phil   A *zero?*

Kev *can't look at him.*

Phil (*to* **Kev** *only*)   I have to get back to Lorna. But rest assured we'll be gone first thing in the morning.

He exits. Sound of front door shutting behind him. Shame and hurt hang heavy in the air. **Kev** *slumps into a chair.*

Kev   I've never felt older.

Jane *drinks.*

Kev   Let's eat something.

Jane   Are you serious?

Kev   Yeah. Let's try and do something normal.

Jane   I'm not hungry.

Kev   Eat something, not talk about any of this, and then get back to it.

Jane   I don't want to eat anything.

Kev   Jane. I think we'll be all right.

She laughs with a freedom that surprises them both.

Jane   I think we're done.

Kev   Don't say that.

Jane   We might possibly eventually be all right if we had a ton of counselling.

Kev   I couldn't do that.

Jane   Why not?

Kev   We'd have to tell them things. I've had it with telling. I never want to be told anything either. Not even the time.

Jane   You'll have to tell Fay something.

He considers.

Kev   I'll tell her I lost my head. That I'm sorry and I made a mistake.

Jane   No you won't. You'll tell her you hadn't the right to tell her you're in love with her, which is different from saying you're not.

Kev   You don't know what I'll tell her and you've no right to instruct me.

She knows he's right.

Jane   It'll only happen again. We'll fall for people again.

Kev   We won't. This has been our vaccination.

Jane   You're never immune.

He knows she's right.

Kev   Let's eat something. Come on. Bit of pasta. Bit of salad. Please.

Jane   OK.

Kev   Will you make a nice dressing?

Jane   I'll make a dressing.

Kev *fills a saucepan with water and puts it on to boil. He gets out a bag of pasta. He takes from the fridge some lettuce, celery, tomatoes.* **Jane** *sets about making a dressing. This activity continues as they speak. Though both feel raw with loneliness, they move about in the kitchen with habitual physical co-operation – two bodies who have shared a cave for a long time.*

Jane   Do you think – I mean apart from all of this – just – when things were normal – do you think we were always just – rubbing along? Or do you think we got somewhere rarer? Higher?

Kev We started high. You can't stay there. We get back up there sometimes. I felt it last summer. I felt full.

Jane When else, recently?

Kev *considers.*

Jane Do you think this is a good marriage?

Kev Yeah. I mean, if the marriage inspectors came today, we wouldn't look too clever, but generally, yeah.

Jane I don't want to be in a bad one.

Kev We love each other don't, we? Like each other?

Jane Have done. Hope so.

Kev I think it's good enough. I don't mean settle for less, I mean good enough as a positive. Sufficiently great, enough of the time.

Jane You really think that?

Kev I really do.

Jane *frowns, absorbs, stirs dressing.*

Kev What's an avocado doing in the egg rack?

Jane I don't know.

Kev Jane. I'm going to look after you. (*He slices the avocado in two.*) This is perfect.

With the knife, he flips the avocado stone into the bin. There is an enormous, reverberating 'clang' as it drops into the empty drum. **Kev** *and* **Jane** *reflexively look up at the ceiling, to* **Jess**'s *room above.*

Jane There's no way she'll sleep through that.

They listen intently.

Kev We'd have heard her by now.

An instantaneous downwards flash appears through the window, of purple feathers and light.

Jane Oh my God!

Kev Jesus!

They fly to the door leading to the yard. They fly out to the yard as soon as the door is open. **Jane** *is heard to cry out. After some moments,* **Kev** *carries a limp and ashen* **Jess** *in his arms, back through the doorway into the kitchen.* **Jane** *follows immediately, aghast, holding her own head with one hand and* **Jess**'s *broken torch in the other.*

Blackout.

A disc of light finds **Jess**'s *face, disembodied, floating strangely high in the darkness.*

Jess (*loud and clear*)
    Dear Mrs Friar,
    I've got some good ideas for lessons. I want the children clever as me to be given harder work, because it's boring waiting for the stupid children like Chistopher. I want to learn to talk Ancient Egypt. Don't you think that sounds fun? I'm going to be a teacher when I'm old and a scientist and a singer. But I'm going to sing the words very clearly. When you a scientist you can find out *everything*. That's what I'm going to do.
    Yours truthfully, Jessica Hammersby.

Blackout.

Scene Five

A telephone rings out mournfully again and again in the dark. Lights up. The kitchen is exactly as **Kev** *and* **Jane** *left it. The telephone continues to ring. Once it finally stops, there's a moment of silence. Then the sound of keys in the lock, followed by approaching footfall.* **Phil** *and* **Lorna** *enter, drunk.*

Phil Let's have a cup of tea first.

Lorna No, let's get it over with.

Phil What's wrong with tomorrow? First thing, before they're up.

Lorna   No. Tonight.

She exits. He pours himself a glass of wine from the open bottle. He has a slug. He sits. He puts his wine down. He gets up to see if there's anything to eat in the saucepan. He's puzzled by finding only water. He taps the sides of the pan to check its temperature. He goes to the box of wine, takes out a bottle, opens it and pours himself a glass. He returns to where he was sitting, reaches to set his wine glass down and notices his first one. He takes a sip from each and stares hard at the room, trying to work it out. **Lorna** *enters, carrying the bag she arrived with.*

Phil   It's like Pompeii. Everything's just been stopped in the middle.

Lorna   I don't think they're in.

Phil   Where would they be?

Lorna   All the lights are on.

Phil (*incredulous*)   They must be in.

Phil *hauls himself up.*

Lorna   I've called a cab.

Phil   Right.

He exits.

Lorna *opens her handbag and plucks out a compact. She rubs colour on her cheeks and lips. Her eyes gleam. She deftly steps out of her underwear and tucks it in the bag.*

Phil *re-enters.*

Phil   Where the fuck could they be?

Lorna   Out.

Phil   Where? In the middle of the night with two babies? There's no note. There's no message . . .

The doorbell rings.

Lorna   That's my cab.

She moves towards her bag. He blocks her way to the door.

Phil   When I came back from Athens when my dad died, Kev picked me up from the airport in his mum's Fiesta.

Lorna   I know darlin'. I know the story.

Phil   And I was so fucked. Very good acid in Athens that year and a young boy from Lanark couldn't say no.

Lorna   I know.

Phil   And I was sweating and scared and he drove me four hundred miles to the funeral and talked to all my aunties and he'd never even met the man.

Lorna   I know.

Phil   Well, you don't know this! Years later – in this kitchen – I told him it was the kindest thing anyone ever did and he shook his head and said when I phoned him from Athens all he could think was how *happy* he was my dad had died because it meant I'd have to come home and life would be interesting again. (*He claps his two hands on his chest.*) Interesting.

Lorna   I know you are.

Phil   SO WHY ARE YOU LEAVING ME?

Lorna   Just let me tell the cab I'm coming.

She darts out. The front door opens.

Lorna (*offstage*)   I'm coming!

Front door shuts. She darts back in.

You are interesting. You're funny. You're kind. You're a fabulous lover.

Phil   Am I a zero?

Lorna   No! You're the nicest man I know, but I don't want to be with you. I want more.

Phil   Where is this more? What is this more?

Lorna   I want to be free to find it.

Phil   You can be with me *and* be free! I don't care!

Lorna   I need to go.

Phil   Listen, *I'd* leave me. But leave me tomorrow.

Lorna *can hardly keep from running out of the door. She craves her destination.*

Lorna   My sister's waiting up!

Phil   Why is this happening now?

Lorna   I just realised it! You know what I'm like, once I know a thing I have to do it!

Phil   When did you realise? Today? Tonight? Is it to do with that guy?

Lorna   No. I have to go. We're too drunk for this.

Phil   You're so lovely. Women are lovely.

Lorna   We're the worst. (*She picks up her bag.*)

Phil   Who's going to glue leather moths on handbags for you at four a.m.?

Lorna   I have to go!

The cab toots.

Bye.

Phil   Kiss me.

Still clutching her bag, she goes to him. His hands hold her low on her hips. They kiss.

Bye-bye.

Lorna   I've never seen you so drunk.

Phil   Good, isn't it?

Lorna   I've got no money.

Swaying, he takes a fold from his back pocket, unpeels some notes and lays them in her hand. She gives him a peck as thanks. She hurries out.

She darts back in.

Forget about other people.

She darts back out.

Sound of front door closing. **Phil** *goes to the box of wine, takes out a bottle, goes to open it, but notices the open bottle standing by the corkscrew. He tracks his glasses of wine down. He has a slug. He sits on the sofa.*

Phil COME HOME WHEREVER YOU ARE!

Keys sound in the door. Footsteps approach. **Jane** *enters. She looks haunted. She carries* **Betty***, in pyjamas, asleep in her arms.* **Jane** *lays* **Betty** *on* **Phil***'s lap. He looks at* **Jane***, scared, waiting for an explanation. A moment.*

Jane (*tears never far away*) Jess is in hospital. Kev's still there. She fell. She was leaning out of her window. I think she was listening. She wanted to know what we were saying and we kept sending her to bed.

Phil Is she bad?

Jane They don't know yet. She's broken some ribs and a wrist. But her head . . . They don't know. I've got to go back. Will you put Betty to bed?

Phil Course.

Jane *starts to hunt for something.*

Jane Have you seen Kev's phone? We'll need it.

Phil *joins the search, ineptly.* **Jane** *happens upon* **Jess***'s letter.*

Jane Oh my God.

She opens the envelope.

'Dear Mrs Friar, I've got some good ideas for lessons.'

She is too upset to carry on. She reads the rest to herself, crying. She looks up.

If she's – if she needs tending to around the clock, that's what I'll do. That's who I'll be.

Phil   She'll be all right.

Jane   Why should she be?

Phil   She will.

Jane   She fell fifteen feet onto stone!

The kitchen telephone rings. **Jane** *seizes it.*

Jane   Kev! . . . What did he tell you? . . . What does that mean? . . . (*She sags to her knees, hanging on to furniture, listening to* **Kev**.) How do they know? What did he say? . . . (*In shock.*) Right. OK. I'm coming straight back . . . OK . . . You too.

She gets up, dazed. She hands the phone to **Phil**.

Phil   Hello, Kev . . . Oh. Thank you . . . Bye.

He puts the phone down.

Jane   It's not certain, but they seem to think she might be fine. Concussed but fine. The consultant said sometimes children fall like cats.

Phil   Fingers crossed.

Jane   (*trembling with tears*)   Isn't luck terrifying?

A dazed silence.

Phone. Phone. Where's his phone.

As she hunts for it.

Did Kev say sorry?

Phil   No.

Jane   What did he say?

Phil   He said, 'I love you.'

Jane   We both do.

She finds **Kev**'s *mobile, holds it up to show* **Phil**. *He holds a thumb up.*

Jane   I'll phone.

Phil   I'll sober up.

Jane   Bye.

She heads out, holding **Kev**'s *phone. Sound of front door opening. Then a distant phone ring. It gets louder as footsteps approach.* **Jane** *re-enters, panicked, holding* **Kev**'s *ringing phone away from her body as if it's on fire.*

Jane   It's Fay! Look! It says 'FAY'!

They stare at the ringing phone. **Phil** *takes it and answers it in one decisive move.*

Phil (*without cruelty*)   Hello Fay! It's not Kev, I'm afraid, it's Phil. I'm his best friend. We met once. I dropped his suit off at your work. I'm sure you don't remember but I was wearing a long-sleeve stripy T-shirt and jeans . . . Because that's what I've worn every day for the last twenty-two years . . . You have a lovely laugh. I remember you very well. Curly hair. Would you call that strawberry blonde? . . . I see. Now listen, here's the rub: Kev is not available. In any sense of the word. (*He looks directly at* **Jane**.) But I am. Freshly available. Abandoned only tonight. (*He takes his eyes away from* **Jane**.) Now, Fay, I want you to focus on the freshness of the abandonment, not the abandonment itself. I don't tend to stay on the shelf very long and I have a lot to offer. (*To and for* **Jane** *again.*) I have a very lot to offer. I am funny, kind, interesting and a fabulous lover according to Lorna. She says she's gone to her sister's but she hasn't. She's run away with the man from Amsterdam and I know that for sure 'cause she's wearing no knickers. (*He looks at the phone, put out.*) So *rude.*

He searches **Jane**'s *face. Did she understand the offer? Has he made a faux pas?* **Jane** *mushes his face in her hands and kisses him hard – like an Italian grandmother – for his friendship, his humour and his own bad luck. The kiss soon ceases to be safe. They kiss with longing and relief. They break for breath and stare at each other – now what? After a moment he holds* **Kev**'s *phone up to her: 'We both know what you have to do, if not for ever, at least for now.' She takes the phone from him. She leaves. Sound of front door closing.*

Phil *reaches for one of his glasses of wine.* **Betty** *stirs.* **Phil** *freezes. She seems to fall back to sleep. He resumes his stretch.* **Betty** *sits bolt upright.*

Betty *(loud and zealous)*   Let me into Heaven, Baby Jesus is my friend!

Phil *freezes again, not sure if she's awake or sleep-talking. She tucks herself back into him and instantly resumes deep sleep. After a moment,* **Phil** *carefully reaches his wine. He drinks. He stares ahead.*

www.ingramcontent.com/pod-product-compliance
Ingram Content Group UK Ltd.
Pitfield, Milton Keynes, MK11 3LW, UK
UKHW040639280225
455688UK00001B/9